THE

HASIDIM

THE HASIDIM

Mystical Adventures and Ecstatics

Anne N. Lowenkopf

SHERBOURNE PRESS, INC.   LOS ANGELES

THE HASIDIM: *Mystical Adventurers and Ecstatics.* Copyright © 1973 by Anne N. Lowenkopf. All rights reserved including the right to reprint in whole or part in any form without prior written permission. Published by Sherbourne Press, Inc. 1640 La Cienega Blvd., Los Angeles, Calif. 90035

ISBN 0-8202-0157-X

FIRST PRINTING

Composition: Omega Repro, Tarzana, Calif.

Printed and bound by R. R. Donnelley & Sons Co., Inc., Crawfordsville, Ind.

CONTENTS

Preface

SOME PEOPLE JUST seem to have a knack. Maybe it's fixing cars or baking pies or mixing socially or administrating heavy work loads. Whatever it is, these are the people who, in their particular line, do twice as much as everyone else, do it better, and seem to get a lot of enjoyment out of the process. They are the ones the rest of us look at half in admiration, half in exasperation, when we are sweaty, baffled, and dog-tired and say to ourselves, "Now, why can't I do that?"

The problem with learning how these people with a knack do it is often that they don't know, or just as frequently the formulations they give us—their tricks of the trade—don't seem to work for others. The best method of learning from them seems to be to watch them closely and, if possible, to work alongside of them. Probably, sad to say, we won't become the experts they are, but we will pick up a better methodology; and, more important, some of their attitudes, some of their feeling for the work that seems to be a crucial factor, may transfer to us so that in the future we see the work differently and we are able to put more of ourselves into it.

Mysticism is no different from driving cars or computing income tax—some people seem to have a knack for it. Today, though people would not admit it about themselves, a good two-thirds of the population care no more for God than they do for vector analysis or Dravidian languages; but even in periods when two-thirds of a society were earnestly striving for a vital relationship with God, some had it and some didn't.

For the moment, ignoring any speculations as to why some have the knack for a relationship with God, let's concentrate on the dilemma of those of us who have the desire but apparently lack the knack. There is a scarcity of genuine mystics to show us the ropes and to provide that little something extra. And with so few models to learn from, it is hard to distinguish a genuine mystic from a fraud.

Secondhand knowledge is not as good as a flesh and blood teacher, but it is a beginning, and the Hasidic mystics have a number of special advantages. The movement produced such a rich harvest that the "study sample" is large enough for us to see how different personality types use different means to accomplish the same goal. Since the modern Hasidic movement is more than two hundred years old, we also have the opportunity to watch how mystics adapt their methods to different environments, and as the Hasidic movement is still continuing, there is the possibility of meeting and learning from flesh and blood mystics—if we are prepared to pay the price connected with following their discipline. So doing also provides us with on-the-scene reports of the human side of the personality of holy men.

Hasidism itself has a special advantage for us in that it comes from the Judaic religion. Because the Jews are and have always been nonevangelical, little is known outside of Judaic circles of the Jewish religion and still less has been known about the riches of Jewish mysticism.

Even within the Jewish community, mystics have been little known, moving invisibly through the patterns of day-to-day life, preferring to keep their holiness hidden from their neighbors and the people who worked with them. Their existence has been inferred from their effects and by chance revelations, but in the main they lived and died unknown.

There is every reason to believe that the founder of Hasidism wished for himself the same anonymity, but the times in which he was born were desperate ones for the Jews, and he was directed to make himself available to his contemporaries. He set the precedent for Jewish mystics living "in the open" where their lives and their teachings could be studied by anyone who wished to. Since then, many others followed his example—the Hasidim.

During the Middle Ages—that golden age of mysticism—holy men and their students from many different religious backgrounds kept in touch with each other, learning, inspiring, taking strength from each other's experiences. Today in the reawakening of interest in mysticism that has come on a worldwide level, the same eagerness to learn from every available source is apparent.

Therefore, I thought an introduction to the Hasidim might be useful today. There is one other reason, however, a simpler and more personal one. By accident, I glimpsed into the life of one of these extraordinary men, found it irresistible, and wanted to read more. A reading list and directory will be found in the appendix for those who wish more than an introduction.

A note about spelling: Hebrew, Yiddish, Russian, and Polish—the languages from which come many of the names and terms we will be using—do not share an alphabet with English. Consequently, the rendering of these names and terms into English spelling varies wildly. As an example, Hasidim can be and has been spelled "Hassidim," "Chasidim," and "Chassidim," as well as "Hasidim," which I finally chose. I used as guidelines for my spelling choices neither linguistic elegance, nor historical research, nor even an intent to be consistent. I have used Hasid (the singular of Hasidim) and Chabad, whereas to have been consistent I should have used Chasid and Chabad or Hasid and Habad.

I chose spelling for easy recognition with other

writings—on the basis of informal frequency counts—and after I finished, I realized that I had failed. All of these spellings are in use in various and differing combinations. There is no hope of ease, but there is of charm. After a lifetime of using a language that has been largely tamed in terms of spelling, there is delight in having to use the imagination to determine whether a new group of letters is hiding an old friend.

The Rebel

IT IS NECESSARY for man always to bear in mind that God is with him always and everywhere; that He is, so to speak, the finest of matter, which is poured everywhere; that He is the master of all that happens in the universe." These are the words of Israel, the Baal Shem Tov, and they provide us with a clue to mystical vision. The mystic looks at the world and sees God. Most of us, even on the Sabbath, even in the most holy of places, look for God and see the world.

This difference is qualitative and significant. Mankind has developed many religions, and these religions possess strikingly different dogmas. Nevertheless, each of them has produced mystics of its own; and past and present, the messages of the world's mystics are awesomely similar. Mystics share another characteristic: the ability to lend their spiritual perceptions so that those who come in contact with them experience in part the vision and rapture that dominate the mystic's existence.

Here the similarities end. Mystics come in both sexes. They achieve their vision of God at any age, from childhood to the last moments before death. Born an aristocrat or pariah, wealthy or poor, robust or sickly, some have altered civilizations, others have died unknown or have passed their knowledge on to a single disciple.

There is reason to believe—including the internal evidence of the Bible—that from its earliest beginnings the Judaic religion has evoked from its followers mysticism of an unusually powerful and dynamic nature. But for reasons of their own, Jewish mystics chose to live and teach in secret. Little is known about their personalities, but the imperative for secrecy is evident. In searching for evidence about their lives, historians have discovered little more than rumors and shadows. Jewish mystics were, and perhaps are, masters of protective coloring. They lived and moved about in their communities unsuspected by their neighbors, their superiors, or even their relatives.

Some of these mystics' teachings have been preserved in the books that constitute the *Kabbalah* and its commentaries. But all authorities agree that due to distortion and deliberate purpose, the deepest mysteries of the Kabbalah have been written down in code. A student requires the help of a master to unravel its secrets.

Against this background of isolation and spiritual elitism, the founder of Hasidism, affectionately called the *Baal Shem Tov* or its abbreviation the *Besht*, must be viewed not only as a mystic but as a revolutionary hero.

In a time and place when scholarship—expressed by memorizing long tracts of religious texts and commenting upon them in a formalized manner—was considered the measure of a man socially and his most significant mark of piety, the Besht dared to explore new methods of finding God. He turned away from books and argument and looked inward and outward to Nature and prayed for guidance. And when he received guidance and when he found methods that worked better than the time-worn forms of scholarship, he shared his discoveries with all who would listen and with all his feet could travel to reach.

In strictly terms the Besht was not the first Hasid. Hasid is a Hebrew word meaning saint or holy man. From ancient times there have been many such men among the Jews, but the Besht was the first to try to make a nation, a world of Hasidim. For him it was not enough to be a saint; he wanted to be a saint in an international community of saints.

Of his personal life we have only the memories of memories. The Besht was a man of words but not of writing. He taught by telling stories, some fancies of his own making, some folk tales known to the grandparents of his listeners, and some incidents from his life. Those stories circulated from village to village across the face of Europe and across the face of time from his disciples to their disciples, finally finding their way into print years after his death. Some may never have been published.

We are certain that among those that were published are accurate accounts of his life, but many have been blurred in the telling, and others are so distorted that the Besht himself would not be able to recognize them as relating to him. The difficulty is we have no way of knowing what is fact and what is distortion. This difficulty does not present a real problem for any but academicians. In talking about his life the Besht was not trying to relate an autobiography but was using these incidents as a vehicle for his teachings. For his purposes, historical detail would be insignificant beside the message and spirit of a story. Fortunately, the spirit and the message have withstood time. And since in this book, to the extent that it is possible, we have made the Besht's purposes ours, biography, teaching, and fables will be mixed together in the hope that from this jumble the Besht and his work will somehow emerge.

His true name was Israel ben Eliezer, Israel the son of Eliezer. All the tales agree that his parents were poor and getting on in years when Israel was born. The accounts of his mother's chastity and goodness were literary conventions of the period, but were probably no less true for that. Poland was the place and the mid-1700s the time. The Besht lived his first forty years in insignificance. The excitement of his struggles was carried under the skin; nothing was visible from outside.

He was orphaned early, and this tragedy may have freed Israel to look at his world from the outside. What he saw—and his opinion has since been confirmed by reports from many differing sources—was a great display of the empty forms of religion, the pretense of piety to achieve social status, a preoccupation with intellectual gamesmanship on the part of religious leaders—all taking place among a people drowning in poverty, fear, terrible suffering, and despair.

However and whenever he came to that view, Israel was an early rebel, a chronic truant, a drifter through odd jobs. His one major act of conformity to the customs of his time was in marrying young, and, after the death of his wife, in remarrying, some say, the daughter of a wealthy rabbi who had a liking for him. However, the rabbi died before he could bequeath unto Israel anything more than the betrothal. The rabbi's son, Israel's brother-in-law, lacked his father's affection for the young man. He was so unenthusiastic that after trying Israel out unsuccessfully on a few degrading jobs, he gave his sister the choice between divorcing Israel or leaving town with him for a distant place where her husband's bumbling ways would not disgrace the family name.

Homeless, the young couple wandered aimlessly. Finally, Israel settled his bride into a hut in a small village in the foothills of the Carpathian Mountains while he camped out in the wilderness in order to obtain the necessary solitude to seek God and find himself. Even then he did not completely cut himself off from human responsibilities. Two or three times a week his wife would hitch a horse to a wagon and drive up into the mountains to meet Israel. Then he would dig clay from a deposit until he had filled the wagon and she would return to the village to sell it to pot makers for enough money to buy food until the next visit.

While Israel hiked in the mountains during the day and slept under the stars at night with his thoughts and the wildlife as his only companions, his spiritual powers took form, slowly growing, awakening a sense of joy in God. There is no documentation of the first time he began having visions; however, he did tell his disciples that visions came to him frequently, sometimes when he was awake, sometimes during his dreams. The prophet Shijah the Shilonite, who had been a rebel himself and the prophet of a new kingdom, came to teach him not only about the means of achieving mysticism but secrets about this world and others, including, some say, the language of animals and plants.

This period was one of great happiness for the Besht, one that he never forgot. It came to an end when his brother-in-law, the young rabbi Gershon, perhaps overcome with guilt over his former treatment of them, perhaps responding to news of his sister's pregnancy, bought a local inn for the young couple to manage, thereby assuring his sister of a stable income. Even then the gesture was tinged with disrespect. Innkeeping in those days was considered a rather disreputable means of earning one's living. Nor was it to Israel's liking; he found being cooped up indoors unpleasant, and for the most part he left its chores to his wife. He missed the mountains, the closeness he experienced there to Nature untouched by man, the isolation from the downward pull of other people's thoughts. However, his happiness over his wife's increased comfort is certain. A number of intimate vignettes of their life together survive. He was devoted to her, and often spoke of his feelings to his disciples.

A mystic and his sweetheart—theirs is a unique love story, but there is little doubt that he did love her ardently, and he respected her opinion enough to listen to her advice. Once, after she had scolded him for losing his temper with some guests, he sent out notes of apology. She died before him, and though urged, he refused to remarry, saying he would share his life with no other woman. He told his disciples that he had hoped to enter heaven in his fleshly form, but since death had robbed him of half his being, he no longer had the power.

Romantic love has not fared well in the annals of

spiritual discovery. The sharpness of the sexual experience has functioned as a distraction and, during periods of puritanical repression, even as a degrading influence on young people's character. For these reasons and perhaps for some personal problems of their own, many religious teachers have disapproved of love between men and women. The Baal Shem Tov is one of the few mystics to demonstrate it is not a hindrance and can be an asset to the search for God and the acquisition of occult powers. His demonstration is the more remarkable because it was made within a society that granted a man sexual rights to his wife's person and both marital partners certain obligations to each other but not the expectation of shared love.

In his society, marriages were arranged to suit the parents' social and economic ambitions. Many times the girl and boy met for the first time at their formal betrothal, and the weddings were often performed on the pair's fifteenth birthdays. Frequently the social and age gaps between bride and groom were wide; wealthy parents sought an affiliation with a family of prestigious background or the acquisition of a vigorous go-getter, or a middle-aged widower indulged himself in a young beauty for a second wife. Even when the two were more equally matched, marriage signaled the beginning of responsibilities and hardships.

The Besht's wife had more than her share of both. All the evidence suggests that she took on the task of supporting the family in addition to caring for and training their two children almost single-handedly in order to provide her husband with the time he needed for his life's work. The effort may have worn away her strength, but it did not daunt her devotion to him or her belief in his holiness. Many are the stories that show her in the face of her brother's derision and their neighbors' disregard filled with calm assurance of Israel's saintliness and keeping her house as though he were a rabbi.

Indirectly, generations of men and women have benefited from their love affair. His marriage taught the Besht and he then taught his followers that happiness is a spiritual asset and that sensory pleasure can be used as a means of lifting one's thoughts and emotions upward spiritually. He told his disciples that a physical pleasure can become a spiritual pleasure if it is experienced with devotion to God; and if it is performed with the intent to worship God, a physical act can at the same time be a religious act. On his death bed the Besht told his son that his soul was holy because on the occasion of his conception when the Besht had joined his wife, the heavens shook.

During the period that his wife kept the inn, Israel crossed the river on the outskirts of their town and hiked into the foothills beyond. The atmosphere was not as beneficial as that of the Carpathian Mountains, but it was an improvement over that of the local synagogue, and it had the advantage of being removed from prying eyes and meddlesome dispositions. He found in the hills a cave large enough to provide him shelter. Often he spent six days at a time there, sleeping little and eating not much more than his wife's bread, returning home to his family in time for the Sabbath.

It seems likely that it was in that cave that the Besht evolved his theory of prayer and discovered the technique of using body movement to assist concentration. The Besht regarded mechanically repeated devotions as a waste of time and, worse, a hypocrisy. They angered him as if the sight of a man cheating himself of an opportunity to approach God were physically painful. More than once he left a synagogue, infuriated by the lackluster worship he found there. Apathetic prayers, he felt, never reached God. He called them wooden and said they could not fly to heaven. Warm, fresh, energetic prayers were the only ones that could reach their goal.

Israel prepared for his devotions like an athlete warming up for a championship match. He began directing his mind to thoughts of God by humming devotional music or chanting psalms and other holy songs. And when he prayed, he enlisted the muscles of his face and body in the effort. Focusing his mind on each word of the prayer, often on each letter of every word, he transformed the prayer into meditation. The practice both availed him of the power associated with those combinations of form and sound and let the meaning of the prayer's content flow into the deeper levels of his consciousness.

Prayer, he felt, was composed of two parts: the outer form—the words and order of the service—and the inner part—the thoughts and emotions of the worshipper. For Israel the outer form was important only in achieving the inner and must always be subservient to it. Years later when he was famous for his holiness, a child interrupted holy services by taking out a reed flute and playing a tune. The boy's father was terrified and the others present indignant; but the Besht saw the devotion that had prompted the boy's behavior and was pleased, telling those present that the child's desire to join in had pierced the cloud that had hung over their efforts.

In the synagogue the Besht made no effort to keep pace with the others. When reproached, he argued: how can you tell a child when he needs to visit his father? His prayers followed the direction of his meditation and he was not aware of the pulsing murmur around him. As he struggled to fix his mind on God, his body thrashed about violently, bending over so far at times that his head was on the same plane as his knees, and observers feared that he was going to fall. After he had achieved his object, the thrashing ceased. He lost awareness of himself. His eyes, open yet not seeing anything in the physical sphere, seemed to bulge out, and his body trembled with the joy of what he was experiencing. His body tremors must have been violent, judging from the stories of objects that had been set shaking when the Besht was at his prayers.

Most of the Baal Shem Tov's methods had been discovered in solitude, but not all of them. Some he discovered in the middle of the most ordinary occupations. At times his wife needed his help; there were chores to be done that a woman was not permitted to do. He had to buy the brandy for their guests and it must be he who slaughtered the animals. Israel, when she could find him, was happy to be useful, but with the growth of his spirituality, as he worked his thoughts kept wandering away from his chores back to God. On one of these occasions Israel was returning in the wagon with flour his wife badly needed to make the un-leavened bread required to celebrate the Passover feast properly. On his way back from the flour mill, halfway up the mountain, their poor old horse died. Miles from help in an area plagued by bands of savage robbers, with the skies overhead threatening rain, Israel felt the only way to save his flour was to pull the wagon himself. The road was steep, however, and he quickly became too exhausted to keep going. Desperate and miserable, he stood by the wagon weeping and crying out to God.

It was then that he had his first vision of the Prophet Elijah, who told Israel his tears and prayers had found favor with God and promised to send a Christian with a wagon up the lonely mountain road to take Israel and the flour home.

More important than the fulfillment of the improbable promise or the having of the vision was the insight it gave Israel that a person need not necessarily be engaged formally in meditation or prayer to reach God. He learned in another context that devotion and concentration were needed, not the outer forms of piety. That lesson is valuable now. It will be valuable in the conceivable future. But when the Baal Shem Tov learned and taught it, the lesson was precious. In Israel's lifetime, grinding toil, sunup to sundown, started early and continued until it and the other effects of extreme poverty killed him. Training to be a rabbi took almost as much effort, certainly as much time, and even more. Young scholars studied days and nights, often actually holding their eyelids up to avoid falling into an exhausted slumber over their books. Their training began when they were small children and still had not been completed by their wedding day. It was a day-long, week-long, year-long attack on memory and logistical dexterity. The boy who trained for religion had little time for the secular. But few families could afford to spare a son from the chancy business of keeping food on the table, and those who could not had few hours for religion.

It was not easy to be a Jew in that century in Poland. More than a hundred years before Israel's birth, the Polish royalty had formally invited the Jews to enter their country for the purpose of taking over the management of feudal commerce and to encourage its industrial and urban development. Management was badly needed. Poland's peasants lacked the required training, and its aristocracy, intent on playing grandiose games of title and position, refused, as they thought of it, to soil their hands by cultivating money, although they desired the wealth and power such cultivation produced.

The invitation was an overt tactic Christian Europe had been employing sub rosa to circumvent the Church's ban on cultivating money by lending cash for a profit. Instead of developing the generosity the Church had hoped for, Christian princes looked the other way as Jews entered their realms to take charge of the business of moneylending. The arrangement was much to the princes' advantage: they had the use of the Jews' skills without the necessity of granting them even so few civil rights as their Christian subjects possessed. Consequently, Europe possessed a large population of Jews who were experienced in the machinations of money and urban life. As a group they were indispensable; as individuals they were useful but expendable, and their value fluctuated with the rise and fall of counselors and treaties of commerce and peace. They lived precarious, painful lives surrounded by an alien culture, and they were a perfect target for scapegoating.

In hopes of a better life, Jews responded to the Polish invitation by the thousands and became the kingdom's rent and tax collectors and estate managers, acting as middlemen between the grasping aristocracy and its impoverished peasantry, earning for themselves in the process contempt and suspicion from their masters and bleak hatred from the wretched masses.

In 1648 the explosion occurred. Polish Jews by the tens of thousands were slain; perhaps more than one hundred thousand were killed in a ten-year period. Some were flayed, some drowned, some buried alive or mutilated; their women were raped and abducted or raped and killed. The lucky ones were able to flee the kingdom losing everything but their skins. Those who survived and remained led lives haunted by terror and the want of basic physical necessities.

One hundred years later the position of the Jews had not improved substantially. Because of their skills, some were once again being used in managerial positions, but most had been pushed to the level of serfs and hated serfs at that.

During the balmy days before the explosion, scholarship had flourished among the prosperous Jewish communities of Poland. A hundred years later in each generation the members of a town who could read and write were few and seemingly growing fewer. Religious leaders had ceased to be a strong force for community welfare. They had withdrawn into dry, scholastic abstractions and endless theoretical bickerings. They had shrunk their world down to a kind of semantic chess game and as long as they kept their attention focused on its strategy, their lives did not seem nightmarish. It was an escape for the learned only, and that escape effectively cut off the majority of the community from any meaningful participation in religious life, leaving them alone and helpless in the nightmare.

When Israel began to teach, he entered into that nightmare with the message that the peasant and villager could find God while they were engaged in the labors that fed their families. He showed them how to make their work a worship, and he presented his ideas in stories and words that even a tired man and woman could understand.

Having progressed in his personal spiritual growth during this period when he was combining his responsibilities as an innkeeper with periods of seclusion, Israel knew that if a person looked, everything he saw or heard, everything he experienced, contained a teaching—a *torah* he called it—for him. He saw life as a steady stream of teachings about God and spiritual endeavor. He said again and again that everything could be a source of learning. Once someone asked him what could be learned from ice. He answered, if the atmosphere is cold and harsh enough, even pure water can be forced into obscene, rigid shapes. But with warmth, with devotion, labor can function as prayer. When you look at material things, he taught, you see in reality the Divine Countenance that is present everywhere. Keeping this in mind, you will find it possible to serve the Lord in all things, even in trifles.

The possibility exists that Israel's occult powers matured before his rapprochement with God was complete. Or it may have been that the occult powers were an outcome of spiritual development he deliberately concealed because he wanted to live alone with God for a time without taking on the responsibilities of spiritual disciples. That desire certainly influenced his behavior. If left to himself, he might have continued dividing his time between the inn and his cave, but shortly before he was forty, the voice of God spoke to him saying, "The time has come for you to reveal yourself."

In obedience to God's command, what he revealed were his occult powers as he traveled from village to village, curing the sick and helping the peasants with their many afflictions. According to the tales, he used physical means when physical means did the job, but when they failed, he applied secret knowledge of how to manipulate the Tetragammaton and other Holy Names. Israel was not the only man in eastern Europe to be using this knowledge. The method of working wonders by manipulation of holy names can be found in the Kabbalistic library, if one looks properly; and in those days the number of men who had unraveled its mysteries was greater than today. Enough practiced this art to give the calling a name—Baal Shem, Master of the Names (of God).

Israel was reputed to be extraordinarily adept in this profession, a man who was called in when others had failed. He was called the Baal Shem Tov. Tov in Hebrew means good and the additional flourish is said by some to be a play on words, implying both that he was skilled and that he was kindly. Among the many Baal Shem, Israel was *the* Baal Shem *Tov*. In time the title became abbreviated to Besht and by this nickname he referred to himself and was called by all except those who could only bring themselves to refer to him as master.

Stories of his cures are legion. At times his prowess made him extremely unpopular with other practitioners, including the rabbis. One rabbi from the town of Ostrog was said to have threatened to kill him with a gun. However, unexpectedly running into the Besht, the best the rabbi could do was demand where Israel had learned medicine. From God, the Besht told him. When the rabbi went to his patient whom the Besht had been treating, he discovered to his chagrin that all he could think to recommend had already been performed; further, the patient had been comforted by Israel's devotion to God and repulsed by his rabbi's lack of devotion.

People came to Israel's town from great distances to be cured, and those too sick to travel sent for him. He took to moving across the countryside of eastern Poland, the word of his route fanning out ahead of him. He made childless women ready to conceive. He restored sanity to those whom life had maddened. They said once in time of drought, he caused the rain to fall. He could see into the future and provide instructions to avert impending calamity. He was known to marvel that those around him could not see the Angel of

Death following a doomed man as he could. And most particularly, he was known for his ability to dispel evil.

It was a period of great evil. Rationalism had not yet killed the study of the occult, but the jealous ravaging of the Church had destroyed the pagan priesthoods that had controlled its use. In consequence of this loss of supervisory control aggravated by the prevailing misery of the age, occult sciences were being practiced recklessly and malevolently for private gain, personal spite, and purposes of group terrorism. Additionally the leaders of both Jewish and Christian religions were haranguing about the varieties of sin, the agonies of hell, and the cleverness with which Satan slicks down the skids that deliver the unwary into his arms. The combination of real and imagined dangers had most of Europe in a state of near hysteria occasionally lapsing into nationwide panic that literally sent people dashing and hollering through the streets or rolling in convulsions on the ground or off in orgies of group lunacy. Periodically epidemics of possession swept through city, town, village, and hamlet; citizens of both sexes and all ages screamed that they were possessed by demons or spirits or due to their atypical and undesirable behavior were thought to be possessed by those around them. Whatever the causal factors these people felt miserable and were unable to fulfill their responsibilities. These disturbances were widespread and vexing enough so that the communities mobilized a variety of means of controlling them: rabbis, priests, professional witch-hunters, as well as Baal Shems, had attempted to provide relief to the possessed and their victims.

Unlike most of his contemporaries, Israel was not afraid of spirits or demons. On one occasion when he was acting as a private tutor for some children, it was reported that the only living quarters available for him were haunted by evil spirits. Not the least perturbed, Israel moved right in, announcing to the spirits that they had best go up to the attic to live and not bother him. Those on the scene said that from time to time, when the house spirits became rowdy, he told them to be quiet, and like children they hushed up for a bit.

Another story describes the appearance of some demons that had been cavorting throughout the house of the local tax collector, making his life a misery. The Besht prepared a number of amulets, instructing his secretary to write certain words on strips of paper. He took the strips and placed them carefully throughout the afflicted house. Knowing what would happen, he left. But neighbors who had stayed to watch said that, in their hurry to flee, the spirits took shapes like a whirlwind, spinning about from room to room and finally rolling out of the house and away.

Contemporary students of the Besht play down his miracle working with the frequently repeated suggestion that the stories of his occult abilities belong to legend. Researching his life, however, the closer one comes to the accounts of those who actually knew him, the more prevalent and more insistent are the stories of his supernatural powers.

Clearly, he believed in his own powers, believed so strongly that he took great pains to insure his prescriptions were followed. Once he foresaw that the son of one of his disciples would drown on a certain day if the boy was allowed to swim in the river. He told the disciple of his vision, warning him to go to any lengths on that day to keep his son from the river. Then he predicted, no doubt from bitter past experience, that the disciple would forget his warning. He told his disciple that on the day of danger he would see his son wearing two socks on one foot. That is the way it happened. One day the son came to his father, one foot bare, looking for a lost sock. After a flurry of searching, the father noticed his son had absent-mindedly put it on top of the other sock on his foot. Then the father remembered that it was indeed the day against which the Besht had warned him and, despite his son's reckless determination to go swimming, was able to keep the boy safe at home.

It seems likely that Israel's visions were of three kinds. One and perhaps the first kind that he had experienced was in the form of a dream. Another, as in the case of the Angel of Death, came as a perception he did not distinguish as being different from "normal" sight. The last was a kind of knowing; suddenly he possessed information he had not had before. Some of this information he could distinguish from the usual means of knowing, and deliberately employed methods to receive it. Once when he wanted to discover whether a certain man's oxen had been stolen, he called for a copy of the Zohar, the famous Kabbalistic Book of Splendor; opening it, he read one of the pages carefully and then told those around him that the oxen were where they belonged. One of his followers asked wonderingly how the Zohar was connected with the information and was told that God had hidden the light by which it is possible to see the world from its beginning to its end in the holy torah of the Zohar. The light is still there, ready for use by righteous individuals, he finished challengingly.

Holy Man and Renegade

2

DESPITE HIS DESIRE to remain inconspicuous, identified as no more than a Baal Shem, little by little those around Israel became aware that he was a mystic as well as a healer, that he had spiritual as well as occult powers, and that he could cure men's souls as well as their bodies. First one then another became aware that a great spiritual force was among them.

One of the early ones to stumble accidentally upon Israel's secret was Rabbi David. He had come to the inn one day while Israel was practicing his devotions. In accordance with Israel's instructions, his wife told the rabbi that Israel was not there to greet him because he had gone to water the tax collector's stock. She served Rabbi David his supper, and after he had eaten, he went to bed, tired from his long journey. He was awakened, however, in the middle of the night by a bright light. Thinking there must be a fire, the rabbi went to investigate. There was no fire. Instead he saw Israel sitting near the oven with a radiance like a rainbow playing down on him. Immediately Rabbi David guessed the significance of what he had seen. He quietly returned to his room, but next morning, he asked Israel about it, brushing aside the Besht's evasive answers. Finally, Israel realized that Rabbi David was too wise to be misled, and confessed. Thereafter every week at the rabbi's insistence, Israel gave him spiritual instructions. For his part, the rabbi kept his promise to Israel to say nothing even when those who listened to his sermons asked where he had learned the teachings he was passing on to them. The one thing he could not do, however, was to keep his silence completely when the Besht's brother-in-law, Rabbi Gershon, scolded Israel. Angrily, Rabbi David would tell Rabbi Gershon to be quiet; he was scolding someone wiser than he.

In the beginning whenever someone discovered Israel's secret, he would be sworn to silence, but ultimately, Israel was pushed out of concealment.

Israel's fame as a healer grew, and so, too, did the number and importance of his visions. One year, he was sitting at his prayers on the first day of Rosh Hashanah (New Year's) when his soul seemed to be lifted out of his body, and he saw the Messiah and many of the souls of the dead in heaven. He called out, "Tell me, Master, when you will appear on earth." The answer came: "When your teachings shall be known and the fountains of your wisdom flow, when all other men shall experience spiritual ascent as you do, then shall all the hosts of impurity disappear and the time of great favor and salvation arrive."

From that time on the Besht taught openly. He flung himself into the effort of raising the spirituality of all he met. Deliberately attracting as many followers as possible, he began training his disciples to go out among the people as he did to stimulate their hunger for God and to show them how to satisfy it.

As never before he traveled the rough roads and dangerous countryside of Poland, visiting distant villages and towns, quickening the mystical powers in an ever-increasing number of men, women, and children. His followers spread the word that there was a great *zaddik* (one who teaches by virtue of his righteousness in God's eyes) and this zaddik would concern himself with the man who worked in the fields and with the cobbler and with the woman trying to make a meal out of bits and drabs of food.

The Besht preached joy because he felt that the souls of his people were weighed down by misery, but part of the exuberance and gaiety of Hasidism came from the relief his followers felt that someone with authority had entered their nightmare world and was showing them a way out. Their stomachs were no fuller, but they had also been starving in a different way, and now they were being nourished.

In time, although not without a long, drawn-out struggle, even Israel's brother-in-law came to recognize his holiness. Rabbi Gershon's habit of underestimating the Besht was an old habit and it went deep. It kept cropping up long after he knew better, so the Besht's followers loved to poke fun at his slips. One such story tells of the time on the eve of Sabbath when Rabbi Gershon asked the Besht why he had taken so long over his prayer, and Israel explained that he had been concentrating on a mystical formula related to the verse "Thou quicken the Dead" when a troop of spirits of the dead came to him in a vision. He began talking to each of them in order to use his mystical force to help them rise to heaven. Hearing this, however, Rabbi Gershon could not believe the Besht had such power and asked why, if what Israel had said was true, the spirits of the dead never came to him. With a smile the Besht had his brother-in-law write some words down on paper, telling him to concentrate on saying the formula and see what happened. The next day Rabbi Gershon followed the Besht's instructions. Suddenly, he had a vision of dozens and dozens of spirits of the dead coming directly at him. The vision was too much for his level of development. He fainted from fear. The Besht, who had expected this very reaction, had been standing nearby to help him when it happened. He revived his brother-in-law, advising him to go home and rest.

Not many years after he had revealed himself, so many people swarmed into the town of Tluste, which had been his headquarters, that the town was unable to provide adequate food and lodging for them. Sometime in the year 1740, the Besht moved with his followers to the larger town of Medziboz. As it was already a place of pilgrimage for rabbis and scholars visiting its ancient synagogue, Medziboz had all the needed conveniences for travelers including roads to Poland, Ukrania, and Lithuania. Down these roads, travelers rode in carriages or on horses, but most of all, they walked, tired and dusty—or muddy—but eager to listen to the words of the Besht.

He told those who came to hear him that everywhere he looked, he saw God. Absence of God is an illusion. His divine glory, the *Shekhinah*, shines forth in all things. At times one may see that God is hiding behind barriers, but if the worshipper pushes forward bravely in his spiritual adventure, he will find no obstacle between himself and his goal. Sin and evil are as illusory as the absence of God. Rabbi Israel preached that even the Evil One himself was part of God's glory and could be used by man as a means toward goodness and virtue. Do not despise sin, he urged, transform it to purity.

Thinking of those rabbis who shut themselves up in their synagogues while their congregations starved or became crazed with fear, the Baal Shem Tov spoke angrily against pride. He had no patience with studying holy texts for the sake of the prestige such scholarship gathered in the community, or with discussing holy matters as an intellectual exercise. But he recognized and encouraged the kind of learning that stimulated piety and pride of the kind that makes a man dare to seek God.

His own humility was not related to niggling matters of precedence but flowed from his continual awareness that he needed God but God did not need him. He once told his grandson that although he heard Torah from God and his Shekhinah, he knew he could fall into foolish ways and be pushed aside. The confidence that shone from the Besht came from his faith in God, not in a delusion of superiority.

The memory of those pathetic souls he had treated in his days as a healer gave him a horror of gloom. Gloom produced hopelessness and meanness. It was a barrier to man's search for God. He would tell the peasants that nothing shut the gates of heaven as does a brooding and melancholy mind. Joy, on the other hand, opens the way to God's grace. He would say, no child is born except through pleasure and joy; by the same token, if one wishes his prayes to bear fruit, he must offer them with pleasure and joy. He felt that the knowledge that life is lived in the midst of God's glory should make man happy and confident.

He believed the Jews had known enough of suffering and privation. He urged them not to mortify their bodies but to purify their senses so that they would come to see God in their daily routine of village life. The Besht wrote one of his disciples, "I hear that you think yourself compelled from religious motives to enter upon a course of penance and prayers. My soul is outraged by your determination. By the counsel of God, I order you to abandon such practices, which are but the outcome of a disordered mind. It is written, 'Thou shalt not hide thyself from thine own flesh!'" In the place of penance and agonizing over sin, again and again, the Besht urged his followers to pray.

Prayer was nothing new to the Judaic religion, but prayers had ceased to be a natural outpouring of the heart like the shepherd songs of David and become rote exercises to be mumbled at prescribed times. Such mumblings invariably caused the Besht to shudder. More than once, he stormed out of a synagogue, unable to endure the mechanical devotions he heard there, declaring, dead prayers are never heard by God. Only worship performed from the heart with enthusiasm is acceptable. When prayers are fresh and rapturous, they help a man to lose his sense of living apart from God.

The kind of prayer the Baal Shem Tov wanted from his disciples was not incantation but meditation accompanied by words and resting on a foundation of genuine emotion. He knew that this type of prayer could not be wished for. It develops only out of spiritual growth. But he believed that spiritual growth could be "fertilized" by the right kind of prayer. He reminded his followers that his own spiritual vision came not in the synagogue or while studying holy texts but during prayer and prayerful work.

As a first exercise in developing the ability to pray inwardly, he suggested preparing to pray by singing or chanting devotional songs that make the heart joyful, concentrating on the words of the song as well as its melody. He agreed with the Kabbalists—on the basis of firsthand knowledge—that the words and letters of certain prayers do have miraculous powers. In fact he would have been considered a Lurian Kabbalist himself if his own innovations were not so important that they focus attention on themselves to the exclusion of other influences. He adopted certain of Isaac Luria's doctrines, and he preferred the Sephardic version of Luria's service to the orthodox service that was customarily used in the synagogues at that time.

To the extent that certain rituals and incantations have an innate power, a mystical or occult energy of their own, he believed in utilizing them. In this sense he advocated scholarship, telling his disciples that those who study the Torah for the sake of making contact with its letters will find their mystical powers increased because the letters of the Torah descended to man from a heavenly source and still contain power from that source.

Unquestionably the Besht believed that the greatest source of mystical power was *devekut*. Devekut is a hard word to translate because English is no longer a language of mystics, and in fact since the Norman Conquest in 1066, English-speaking mystics have been few. Devekut implies not quite the union with God that is the goal of Far Eastern religions because with devekut there is no merging, no loss of personality; it is more a clinging, an adhesion—the self is forgotten but not lost.

Although the Besht believed that, ultimately, devekut

was the gift of God and that the decision to give was God's, not man's, he did not think the worshipper had to be completely passive. Prayer can attract God's attention, but prayer in itself is nothing unless the worshipper's attention is focused on God. This focusing of attention is called in Hebrew, *kavanah;* it is similar to concentration or meditative thought, but it also implies a more ongoing process. The more kavanah in one's prayers and daily life, the more likely God will be to grant devekut. The Besht believed that faith was nothing more than devekut and that this clinging to God could encompass all personal relationships and activities.

Having learned from his own struggles that kinetic motion evokes emotion as well as expresses it, the Besht urged his disciples to move their bodies passionately while they prayed and to speak out their prayers in a loud voice. He believed that the best prayer is one that moves the body as well as the soul, quoting the line, "All my bones shall say, Lord, who is like unto thee." He assured his followers that when gloom and depression threatened to overwhelm them, this method would attract God's attention.

Believing that God's Shekhinah was in all things, the Besht emphasized the Shekhinah in man. Each of you, he told his followers, is a limb of the Shekhinah. He yearned for the appointed hour when the Messiah will come, not because the coming will end human misery but because then true unity with God will become possible. All souls will flow back into their source which is God.

The Baal Shem Tov did not, however, believe in the equality of souls. He accepted Isaac Luria's theory that while every soul is energized by the divine sparks of the holy Shekhinah, the number of sparks of divinity (or the amount of emanation) contained within the soul varies from person to person.

While this theory would seem to explain the obvious differences in spirituality that exist among people, it also implies that many persons are incapable of anything more than a very limited spiritual development. This reasoning may have been related to the sense of dismay he experienced upon hearing in his great vision the conditions the Messiah set forth. However, the Besht's behavior suggests that he did not accept fully such an implication. He reached out to everyone who would listen to him. He is not known ever to have said that a man was beyond redemption.

The Besht was not impressed by past mistakes. He was interested in men and women who were willing to make the effort to achieve devekut. And there was something within him that had the ability to stir up or create the desire to serve God. He used the power of his own devotion to quicken the latent spirituality of those around him. He helped the divine sparks within their own souls to rise to God. Giving this aid, in fact, was what he was doing that caused him to delay in his prayers the day that he had his vision of the souls of the dead. He was attempting to give spiritual energy to each of the souls he talked to. His success on that occasion may be open to question, but his ability to vivify the mystical lives of ordinary people he met was known to his contemporaries. Contact with him manifested seemingly nonexistent spirituality and magnified the efforts of those already engaged in spiritual pursuits.

It was as a result of his success that he developed his theory about the role of the zaddik in spiritual development. The word zaddik predated Israel in the Jewish community and was used to refer to a teacher who was righteous and whose authority came from God. The Besht made the word more specific. He felt a zaddik was indeed righteous; he was a man who contained more divine sparks in his soul than other men. His power radiates outward, lighting up not only his own devotion but his daily trivial acts and the devotion and behavior of others. It is the duty of such a man to lead his people toward God; to teach them how to attach themselves to God; and when they are incapable of making progress by themselves, to use their mystical power to overcome their difficulties until they can go forward by themselves.

Because of his sense of obligation to others, even after he had become famous, he moved intimately among peasants and villagers, talking with them, living with them. He believed that in this way he could make his influence accomplish the most good. He did not drape his holiness with robes and enshrine it in a synagogue. He gave his torah in the marketplace or in a peasant's hut, while he sat, pipe in hand, dressed like any other man, and spoke his torah in simple country language.

He knew that, while he raised the souls of those in the marketplace, the marketplace was at the same time exerting its effect on him. And he was never so proud that he felt immune from the downward pull of negative thoughts and emotions. He kept himself constantly alert for such influences, and he had confidence that God would lift him up if he fell.

He told his followers that in order to benefit most from a zaddik's care, they must give him their hearts and their trust. In those periods when their zaddik seems to have lost his way and becomes mired in the pitfalls of the world, they must remember that the zaddik has deliberately put himself in jeopardy in order to help them. Instead of a splendid and secure isolation, the zaddik puts himself in the center of the community with all its temptations so that he may lift up the community's spiritual level.

The Besht required of the zaddik a similar confidence in his followers. The zaddik must not think of his followers as sinners. He must concentrate his attention on the divine sparks within the man rather than on his weaknesses. When the Besht heard a rabbi or preacher stretching forth a list of sins of the Jews, he became very angry. He felt that the religious leaders should call to the attention of God and of the people themselves their good qualities and their sufferings. He himself looked with sympathy even on a heretic whose very name drew curses from those around him. And he taught his disciples to follow his example, to pray for their enemies, and to see the holy Shekhinah in everybody as well as in all things.

These were the teachings that made Medziboz a place of pilgrimage during his life and after. If his torah drew people out of their huts and mansions, pulling them toward Medziboz, they also drew fiery opposition from the community's rabbinical leadership. The very appeal of his teachings, the enthusiastic response to them by the usually indifferent and mundane made the rabbis suspicious of this new phenomenon in their midst.

It is easy to scoff at their suspicions as masked jealousy. No doubt they were jealous—rabbis have human emotions— and the Besht had emptied their pews, leaving their synagogues with a forlorn showing of capped heads. No doubt guilt over their own negligence and snobbery influenced their judgment, but they had other reasons as well. The rabbis had heard of the mass enthusiasm followed by faith-destroying trauma that had welcomed the preachings of the infamous charlatans Sabbatai Zevi and Jacob Frank and feared that this new wild man might inflict similar harm on their communities. How could even those who were not religious frauds and hypocrites have confidence in a man who spoke so vehemently against talmudic scholarship, decorous participation in the synagogue's services, and the necessity of penitential fasting? The Besht's teachings were shaking the foundation of their tight, secure little world. And he dressed and talked like a peasant. And he consorted with low people. And he was so noisy and violent in his prayers. And the things he said—they were outrageous, radical, dangerous.

The rabbis saw him as offensive, as a threat to cherished beliefs and a comfortable way of life, and as a renegade who would betray Judaism. They grumbled to each other and warned their congregations that the Besht was a false prophet.

To the peasants and villagers, however, he was a god-send; and perhaps actually he was. There had been a century of misery for the Jews in Poland. And if the hatred and oppression they suffered daily from their Christian masters was not bad enough, they were harassed by their own religious leaders, told that their sufferings were God's punishment for their sins, tormented with warnings of devilish retribution, until their lives were gripped with fear from within and from without.

The Besht's doctrine that the zaddik refuses to see his followers as sinners was not a matter of words with him. He spoke with anyone who would listen and welcomed all seekers regardless of their past lives. He told the villagers not to worry about their sins—he would attend to them; let them concentrate on loving God. In his preaching from town to town, he dramatized continually his readiness to intercede with God when He was judging the Jews. One such time the Besht was in the midst of his prayers when suddenly he stopped, dashed out to the street, and bought a load of wood from a Christian peddler. The Besht told his disciples to pay for the wood and to give the Christian a glass of brandy for his trouble.

Struck by the Besht's generosity, the Christian blessed the "God of the Jews who created such a holy people." After the peddler had drunk his brandy and left, his disciples asked the Besht why he had interrupted his prayers for such a trivial chore. He told them that while he was praying, he had a vision in which he saw an accusation made against Jewish villagers for cheating Christians. He had rushed outside to obtain a blessing for the Jews by a Christian and so silence the accuser.

As he interceded for the souls of the living and the dead, so he urged his followers to be honest and fair in their dealings, and kind and forgiving to each other. Stories of light and fire radiating from his body are many, but the most important emanation from his person, other than his holiness—perhaps part and parcel of that holiness—was compassion. A poor man all his life, the Besht was always a giver. In later years, regardless of how much was given to him, he never amassed money because he never kept any. What came to him he passed on to the hungry and cold. When he heard of a family in need of money to ransom a prisoner or captive, immediately he began collecting money for that purpose. And he gave more generously with his emotions than with money. The Besht gave love and tenderness; he gave concern and involvement; and most important in those grim days, he gave joy.

In the twentieth century we have seen too many convincing demonstrations of the brutalizing effects of extreme poverty. In the eighteenth century an entire continent was afflicted by poverty and its degrading effects. Chronic misery does make humans indifferent to the misery of others. Brutality is passed along from person to person and seems to grow more violent in the transfer. By example and by the pouring out of love, the Besht fought indifference and apathy and brutality all his life. He encouraged his followers to form a brotherhood of men and women who felt and behaved as though their brotherhood was a biological fact, watching out for each other, sharing with each other, encouraging each other. He showed his followers that this type of communal life strengthened their happiness and even their material welfare.

Just when or how this brotherhood came to be called Hasidim (or its singular, Hasid) is not known. The fact that they were given this name does indicate how the Baal Shem Tov and his followers were regarded by the people of their own time. Hasid is a Hebrew word that from far back in their history the Jews have reserved for a very special kind of mystic: a man loved for his holiness and goodness and revered for his powers.

The mysticism of the Besht may have shown forth in a holy light from time to time, but his goodness and compassion were manifested as gaiety. He gave back laughter and song and dancing to the countryside. He gladdened the hearts of his followers and taught them that true piety does not have to be solemn or sorrowing. Unlike so many religious leaders, he did not begrudge those around him their trivial pleasures. He knew they were not ready to remain always on the upper levels of devekut, and he believed that pleasure and laughter would give them the strength and energy to continue reaching upward in their devotional exercises.

Most of his closest disciples came to him as young men. Instead of trying to squash their youthful exuberance as conventional religious training did, forcing the young rabbi to mimic the ways of an old man, the Besht channeled that enthusiasm into the spiritual adventure. He encouraged his young disciples to shout out their love for God, to leap in the air, to somersault in the excitement of serving God. And in the evening when the young men liked to get together to talk and dream and dance and do a little drinking, he showed them by his smiling face that this too was part of the life of the spirit. The Shekhinah was with them as they danced and sang; the Shekhinah did not flee when they lit their pipes and sipped their brandy. There is a story about a night when, grumpy with his disciples for staying long and boisterously into the night, his wife fussed with the Besht, complaining they were drinking all her wine. She asked him to make them stop and go home. "No," he told her. "You make them stop." Doubly angry, she stomped downstairs. A few minutes later, she was back, a sheepish expression on her face, and downstairs the fun was going on as loud as ever. "Well," demanded her husband, with a twinkling eye. "Did you stop them?"

The joy of the young Hasidic brothers outraged most of the community. There are always those sobersides who become instantly angry on watching another's enjoyment. And in those days when joy and fun were as rare as meat in their soup, disapproval of Hasidic gaiety became fashionable.

When the Besht first began teaching, the orthodox rabbis, if they bothered to notice him at all, laughed at his peasant speech and grotesque contortions during prayer. But as more and more people were discovering that his methods enabled a worshipper to concentrate on God despite an exhausted body, the rabbis began scoffing at the Besht's lack of scholarship. As the roads leading to Medziboz became traveled by more and more people wanting to hear torah from the Besht, their attacks turned desperate and bitter. They accused the Besht of being a fraud; they condemned his methods; and some even charged him with lewd and immoral behavior.

Unperturbed, the Besht followed his own counsel and the commands he received in his visions, often innocently providing his enemies with ammunition for their attacks. He was not interested in people's past lives but in their current behavior. He even used his influence to protect an adulterous woman by persuading her brothers not to kill her in revenge for the shame that she had brought to their name, and he accepted the woman without prejudice into his community. The howls from the self-righteous rang from village to village across the countryside.

The attacks on the person and teachings of the Baal Shem Tov were not strange. What does seem strange, almost miraculous, was his ability to transform a bitter enemy into an ardent disciple in a matter of minutes. The Besht used this kind of spiritual sleight of hand to bring into the Hasidic brotherhood its first writer, the man most responsible for preserving the Besht's teachings.

His name was Jacob Joseph ben Zevi ha-Kohen Katz. The heir of a long and respected rabbinical genealogy, Jacob Joseph was already a rabbi when the Besht first became aware of him—a rabbi with a synagogue of his own and a reputation for learning that had attracted the correspondence of important scholars throughout Poland, a rabbi who was daily denouncing the Besht in brilliant harangues of scorn and vituperation, a rabbi who stood in the forefront of the forces opposing him.

Instead of being angry, the Besht admired Jacob Joseph, perceiving that his passion was a measure of the devotion he had to give to God. Such a man the Besht wanted for his own and he began plotting to abduct this militant mouthpiece of orthodoxy. First, he had to capture his attention. Accordingly, early one morning the Besht traveled to the town in which Jacob Joseph lived and planted himself strategically in the marketplace along the main route to his intended victim's synagogue. When the first of the worshippers approached, the Besht stopped him with a word or two that quickly linked together in one of his stories. The worshipper walked no farther. When the next came by and the next and the next, they paused out of curiosity and were caught.

As the moment for services arrived, Rabbi Joseph entered the worship hall of his synagogue, and instead of the usual sea of *yarmulkes* and prayer shawls, he saw empty chairs. There was not even a *minyan,* the quorum of ten adult males needed to begin the services. His tempestuous temper already stirring, and more than a little puzzled, Rabbi Joseph ordered his *shamus* to go through the town and discover what was causing his congregation to shun their religious obligations.

The shamus found the cause easily enough, but then he too was caught. At length, when the Besht felt his purpose had been served, he suggested to his audience that they all go to the synagogue for the service.

By this time Jacob Joseph was in a rage. He hurried through the service and as soon as the last prayer had been completed, he marched up to the smiling stranger, demanding to know by what right and for what reason he had delayed the Lord's worship. In reply the Besht gave him a story, and then another, and another. . . .

The sorcery won the Besht an invitation to Jacob Joseph's house, and he left town with a new disciple.

Rabbi Joseph did not inform his congregation of his conversion, knowing they would not accept an overnight change of heart. Instead he planned, little by little, to incorporate the Besht's teachings into his own torah and so gradually bring his charges to the place where he had jumped in a single leap. The hitch was that a passionate man like Jacob Joseph is incapable of successful deception. Overnight the melancholy of a lifetime vanished. His bleak attack on prayer was replaced with boisterous, body-swaying exclamations of joy and confidence. His congregation was chattering among themselves like birds in a tree, and then various people began reporting that they had seen their rabbi sneaking out of his house like a thief—or a lover—in the black of night. Unable to endure the mystery, two of the worst busybodies spied on him, following him out of his house and out of town, ending up in front of the house of the notorious Baal Shem Tov, only recently reputed by their rabbi to be the father of evil.

When the news came back, the congregation was overwhelmed with complex, seething emotions, but they found a single expression for them. Rabbi Jacob Joseph was sent packing: they stopped his salary, hooted him when he tried to perform the services, and made his comings and goings a public mockery. It is not impossible that had he remained, they would have stoned him.

Rabbi Joseph moved his family to Raskov. The story of his conversion followed him and the Josephs were harried out of Raskov on their way to a new town that had not heard of the scandal. For years Rabbi Joseph was hounded by his conversion. Just as he and his family were settling into a community, rumors that he was secretly a Hasid began, driving them off. Finally, disgust for the people of Poland grew great within Jacob Joseph. He resolved to leave the land of cruel bigotry and move to Israel. There he hoped to find a place for his family where he could function both as a rabbi and a Hasid, but, if that was not to be, at least he would have the comfort of being persecuted on holy soil.

The Besht, as it happened, had other plans for him. Jacob Joseph tried to be resolute in his determination to leave Poland, but his inability to resist the Besht was already an established fact. With no hope for the future, Jacob Joseph abandoned himself to his master's wishes.

As it often happens among men of God, not long after he made this submission, his troubles came to an end. Leaders from the town of Niemerov contacted him, urging him to come and take charge of their synagogue. Niemerov was a very large town, or a small city, and its Jewish community was already steeped in the mysticism of Kabbalah. Rabbi Joseph's words found ready listeners, and quickly he developed a following that grew large and more adoring as he taught.

Following his master's example, as his spiritual powers grew, Jacob Joseph put them to the use of his people and became known for his healing as well as for his holiness. Jews and Christians alike sought his help. As much of his small salary as his family could spare he used to finance missionary trips, traveling up and down founding Hasidic centers, encouraging those already established; and when he could not go in person, he wrote letters to the Hasidic communities, making himself a communication center for information and comfort.

Eventually his reputation brought him an invitation to take charge of the synagogue in Polna, a large city, strategically located near many Jewish communities.

Polna became the center of Jacob Joseph's missionary work. And it was there that he wrote the books containing the Besht's sayings and teachings. Throughout the worst of the persecution that surrounded him and his followers, the Besht was loved by his disciples more passionately than he was hated by his enemies. For every malicious lie whispered about him, there were two fables being circulated that celebrated his holiness.

One goes all the way back in time to the Garden of Eden. It seems that, anticipating Adam's intention of eating the fruit God had forbidden him, a number of more obedient souls fled in horror and did not stop until they had passed beyond the boundaries of heaven; in so doing, they absolved themselves from culpability and escaped contamination when the ruinous act took place. One of these souls was born as the Besht and that explains why he came into the world in a state of unmarred innocence.

Of the many tales surrounding his conception and birth, one describes how the Prophet Elijah, dressed in rags, came begging at his father's door, negligently toting a traveling staff and knapsack, even though it was the Sabbath, the day on which it is forbidden to travel. But, refusing to pass judgment on another, Eliezer put his arm around the beggar's dirty shoulders, drew him into his hut, shared his food with him, and made him welcome for the night. When morning came, Eliezer himself guided the beggar through town and, taking him to the road he wanted to travel, slipped a coin into his hand while he was saying good-bye. Then Elijah revealed himself, promising Eliezer that he and his wife—this tale has the couple in their hundreds—would be blessed by the birth of a son whom he should name Israel, for this boy was destined to be a light unto his people.

Another story shows Israel as a young man attacked by Satan in the form of a werewolf. Remembering that he need fear nothing but God, Israel seized a stick and drove the Evil One away.

Our favorite story places Israel back in the Carpathian Mountains, a band of robbers watching him, waiting for a good opportunity to rob and kill him. Israel was walking across a high narrow mountain ridge, lost in prayer, too preoccupied to notice that he was heading for a sheer drop into a steep ravine. The robbers chuckled, thinking they would not need to kill him. All they would have to do is climb down and take the coins out of a dead man's pockets. But even as they watched, the mountains moved to close the gap, making a safe passage for Israel's feet.

Dozens of legends spring from his days as a healer. In

that busy period it was said that the Besht was able to sense a family's need for him and travel mysteriously across great distances. Once, however, he arrived too late and a young bride lay dead in the arms of her weeping bridegroom; but the Baal Shem Tov took pity on the young couple and raised the bride up to the world of the living.

Even after he had concentrated his energies on fulfilling the conditions the Messiah set forth for the Galuth, Israel never completely stopped his healing activity. But when his own fatal sickness struck, he looked upon it as a release rather than a disease. He had kept faith with his vision and the time had come to turn the work over to others.

The life of Israel Baal Shem Tov began draining away during the Passover festival. It was said that God had wished to honor him by bringing Israel up to heaven in a fiery chariot but concluded that his generation was unworthy of such a miracle. Instead He granted Israel the ability to keep his powers over the three worlds until his last sighing breath.

In 1760 on the first day of the Feast of Shabuoth, sixty years after his birth, the clocks in his house stopped ticking. The Angel of Death, having received from the Besht his nod of permission, scooped him up in his arms to carry him to the throne of God.

Each of us must decide which of the stories about the Besht is biographical and which is fable. As for us, we have discussed these incidents many times. Some we believe; some we wish to believe; and some we are still debating. One thing is certain, even in this rationalistic age, we do not wish to say certainly that this or that is impossible to God. And even rationalists must admit that often a legend tells the truth more brightly than a dry enumeration of facts.

The greatest miracle performed by Israel, the Baal Shem Tov, was the inception of the Hasidic brotherhood. The brotherhood transformed his vision into a form we all can see and use. Through it he set in motion the fulfillment of the conditions set for him in his great vision. His power was such that the brotherhood has survived the opposition of entrenched authority. It has survived his death. It has survived one of the most hideous blood baths the world has ever seen. It has survived an age of materialism and religious indifference and is even now quickening a spiritual revival. The Hasidic brotherhood was his greatest wonder of all and the brotherhood still exists for all of us to see.

3

Burning Words
and Burning Books

ACCORDING TO THE formal histories of the movement, for six years after the Besht's death, the Hasidic leadership was not assumed by one man. The truth is, the Besht was succeeded by the brotherhood and never by one man.

Nothing could have been more appropriate.

The Besht was irreplaceable. He was one of those rare souls who grace humanity once in a great while, lighting and lifting the world about them, and then disappearing, perhaps to give the rest of us a chance to apply the lessons they taught and lived.

Within the brotherhood the Besht had left behind all of his qualities: his devotion to God, his occult powers, his love of others, his ability to concentrate his thoughts, his unpretentiousness—all of these were present. But no one individual possessed them all. Each member had a combination that was uniquely his own, and each member made his own contribution to the brotherhood and the community.

When the Besht had begun gathering together his brotherhood, his intent had been to create a kind of suprafamily to encourage his disciples to love each other and to help each other love God. He had no intention of founding a formal order bound by rigid rules. The Besht was against rigidity and form; God himself is not bound by form. It is easy to regulate the body, but it was the heart and mind that he sought to capture. Just as he could see no value in fixed periods of prayer and just as he valued devekut more than ritual, so he considered individuality more precious than regulations and the service that a man accomplished more important than title.

But always, inevitably, those who have less power are more interested in form, and those who, due to their own limitations, serve less are more concerned with title. It was no different in the brotherhood.

There was a time of confusion and stumbling following his death. The rawness of loss lay heavily upon his followers. For comfort they gathered around the Besht's son Zevi ben Israel.

Zevi had inherited his father's devotion to God, his kindliness, and his simplicity, but none of his abilities as a leader. It is doubtful that he felt comfortable with the responsibility of leadership. However, the disciples of the Besht assumed he would carry on for his father and he, out of love for the Besht, did the best he could. Nevertheless, it was not enough; the disciples were struggling without direction. One night his father came to Zevi in a dream, or so he reported to the brotherhood, telling him what he knew in his heart, that leadership did not express or fulfill his character and that the brotherhood should find another for that role and let him be.

The dream gave Zevi the courage publicly to announce his intention to resign and enjoy his inheritance of a private life.

Within the brotherhood, however, the immediate result of the dream was conflict and rancor.

Two of Israel's disciples felt themselves to be his obvious successor. For a time they competed with each other, tugging at their brothers' loyalties. From this time distance, it is an interesting struggle due both to their differences and their similarities.

One of the combatants—Jacob Joseph—we have already

met briefly. And combatant is a good description of him; all his life Jacob Joseph fought fiercely for what he believed in. Hypocrisy or half measures were not in him. He was one of the Besht's senior disciples and an ardent Hasidic missionary. In his heart he knew he was the man most devoted to the Besht and most committed to preserving the brotherhood for the function the Besht had envisioned: fulfilling the conditions for ending the Galuth. And so he assumed that the brotherhood would want him to become its leader and zaddik.

This was an instance when Jacob Joseph's personality worked against him. The fury with which he first had attacked the Hasidim was with him still. His feeling about the Besht and his torah had changed, not his stormy temperament. The Besht had been able to see through his bad temper and harsh ways to the equally intense love within, but few men, even among his disciples, had the Besht's ability to read character (which some said was a gift from the Shekhinah at the time of his great vision).

Over the years Rabbi Joseph's sharp tongue and burning eyes had angered and repulsed many of his brother Hasidim. When the time came to choose, they chose against him.

He was angered and hurt by the decision. When Dov Baer, the man the brotherhood accepted as their leader, decided to move the Hasidic headquarters away from the town that the Besht had made famous to his own town, Jacob Joseph's temper flared, and he refused to visit the headquarters or Dov Baer.

In a sense the enemies of the Hasidim healed their quarrel. Now that the Besht and his magical ability to subdue anger were gone, the orthodoxy was attacking the brotherhood on all sides. The movement was slandered. Hasidim were refused entrance to their local synagogues. And even their children were pointed at and shunned by the children from orthodox families.

As soon as he realized that the brotherhood was being

persecuted from without and was floundering from divided loyalties, Jacob Joseph's anger at Dov Baer evaporated in the heat of his concern. He approached Dov Baer, offering him the use of his literary talents and his reputation. The two men discussed the tactics of survival and growth and from that moment on, they never ceased cooperating with each other for the communal good.

The responsibility to hold the brotherhood together belonged to Dov Baer, but Jacob Joseph felt a need to further the Hasidic cause in some way. He began writing down from memory the Besht's torah and his own understanding of what the Besht's words meant. Twenty years after the death of his master, Jacob Joseph's first book, *Toledot Ya' akov Yosef,* was published. It was a rich stew of "words which I heard from my teacher," the essence of the Besht's viewpoints told in homilies, and interpretations of the Bible, as well as spleen-venting attacks on the rabbinical establishment that he characterized as Jewish devils the equal of Satan and the manifestation of evil itself. In his diatribe, he charged that the rabbis were motivated by money hunger, that they wrung coin from near-starving peasants in order to keep themselves and their families in luxury, and that their preaching was designed to overawe rather than to inspire.

From the beginning the book was an enormous success with its intended audience, the men and women who sought a guide out of stylized ritual into the realm of mysticism. Not surprisingly the orthodox rabbis and their supporters were less than pleased with Jacob Joseph's comments. Denouncements, roars of fury, and written invectives followed the book's appearance. Often the book was condemned within the temple of God. Occasionally it was burned formally in front of the temple.

Despite the furor it caused, the book continued to be read. Often its readers had first heard of it in the tirades of its opponents. In 1781 Jacob Joseph published his second book, *Ben Parat Yosef* [Another Book by Joseph], this time applying Hasidic interpretation to the Book of Genesis. In it he included a letter that the Besht had sent his brother-in-law in 1750, providing the world with a sample of writing authored by the Baal Shem Tov that may be unique.

Zafenot Pa' ne' ah [Revealer of Secrets], his commentary on Exodus, was brought out in 1782; and forty-four years later, so long a delay that for many years the book was considered a forgery, his commentary on Leviticus and Numbers, *Ketonet Passim* [A Coat of Many Colors], was published.

It is impossible that Jacob Joseph's writing could exactly duplicate the Besht's teachings. Two people, however close, interpret the same words and phrases differently, and the words Jacob Joseph wrote had been altered by time as well as personality. One tale about the Besht points up the literary problem, recounting the time Israel discovered one of his disciples writing down his torah and, looking at what had been written, declared sadly, "Nothing that I have taught is down here."

Nevertheless, the intent to reproduce his master's torah faithfully was strong in Jacob Joseph and his writings ring true with reports of his master's message from other sources. His books, with such distortions as they may have, are important because the message of a great mystic has come down to us in a way that can be verified as having been written by a close disciple. In his books Jacob Joseph wrote that the most important teaching of all and man's ultimate purpose is, You shall cling to Him.

Completely turning his back on his former scholasticism, he points out that devotion to God—devekut—could be achieved not through fasting and self-mortification or memorizing books, but through joy. He warns his readers that sorrow is the root of all evil. And what need is there for sorrow, he asks, when God is present everywhere and in every human thought?

When his Hasid brothers came to him, worried because

their thoughts had wandered in sordid ways while they were praying, Jacob Joseph comforted them with the explanation that they were being given an opportunity. Even in evil thoughts the divine sparks of the Shekhinah exist. When those thoughts come to the mind during prayer, the worshipper has the chance to improve them and free the divine sparks to lift toward God. Evil inclinations can be converted into a tool for good by combining sensuous joy with the spiritual form of prayer.

Rabbi Joseph saw the ideal community as a living organism. The zaddik should act as its head and eyes while the great mass of the community functions as its feet. This concept is undemocratic, but it has the virtue of giving hope to those who feared only the fortunate were elected by God to reach Him, the rest being condemned to fail however earnest their attempt. Because leader and community belong to one spiritual body, Jacob Joseph taught, no one member could achieve complete redemption until all have been redeemed.

He was aware that the poor had no time to give to study and little for prayer, but, he maintained, this lack was no hindrance to their spiritual goals. A man who clung to his zaddik had no need to be a scholar. It seems fair to say that Jacob Joseph believed the zaddik acts as a redeemer until the Messiah comes. He had witnessed the Besht's ability to persuade God to change a harsh judgment to a favorable one, and he had witnessed his ability to lift up the thoughts and behavior of his followers. He had come to the conclusion that the zaddik was the vital core of the brotherhood; it is notable that he refused to establish his own dynastic line. As far as Jacob Joseph was concerned, Dov Baer was the zaddik for the brotherhood. He encouraged his Hasidic brothers to give Dov Baer devotion and loyalty. It was he who was the first to emphasize the importance of all the members of the brotherhood joining their zaddik for the third meal on the Sabbath, telling them that the man who failed to keep this communion profaned his Sabbath. Next to God himself, Jacob Joseph taught, the zaddik should be the object of men's devotion. He was a man who lived his teachings. He gave his allegiance fully to Dov Baer and eventually found it in his heart to write that after the death of Rabbi Israel Baal Shem Tov, the Shekhinah moved with knapsack and staff from Medziboz and chose Meseritz as its abode.

4

The Maggid of Merteritz

IT IS SAID that one midnight, following the Besht's orders, one of his disciples ushered a dour-looking individual into his room. The disciple could not understand why the Besht wanted to meet the man; he seemed to represent everything he most disliked in religious leadership. The newcomer's body was emaciated and sickened by the excesses of Lurianic penance. His speech dripped the set phrases of talmudic learning. His attitude was haughty and severe.

Pain and chronic invalidism rather than desire to learn brought the stranger, Dov Baer, to the Besht. He had tried everything else, but each day his health seemed to grow worse. He felt weak. He was in constant pain. A mysterious disease was attacking his legs, making walking without help impossible and even standing difficult. At last he had given in to those who had been urging him for some time to visit the famous healer. However, earlier that afternoon, repelled by the Besht's appearance and earthy conversation, he had turned away without speaking, making his way slowly through the crowd surrounding the Besht, resolved to leave town in the morning.

The invitation was another case of the Besht deciding to convert an enemy into a disciple. And the strange hour for the initial meeting was one of his attention-getters.

Having succeeded in catching Dov Baer's attention, the

Besht followed through with a deft question about a passage in a mystical text. Glibly, Dov Baer rattled off the customary scholastic interpretation. The Besht smilingly disagreed, telling him he had remembered the words correctly but had failed to master the text's inner meaning. Then he began explaining the meaning behind the surface of the paragraph and as he spoke, it is said, the radiance from his face lit up the darkened room.

That night there was no sleep for the invalid. He and his new master bent over the text together, discussing, studying, meditating, until the words of the manuscript glowed like shining seraphim.

Dov Baer had been born in the Volhynian village of Lutatsch. Abraham, his father, was bleakly poor, but he was a teacher, and the blood of scholars flowed in his veins. He passed the inheritance along to his son. From the moment the local rabbi began teaching little Dov Baer, the child studied as though he were running a race with time. Angry that long hours and small print closed his eyes in spite of his desire to stay awake, he discovered that by studying on his feet, he could keep going longer. Soon his feet hurt all the time and walking began to be painful, but his efforts had captured the imagination of the villagers, and they all contributed a little money to send their young scholar to Lemberg, an important center of religious learning.

The boy responded to the opportunity and his new independence by shortening his hours of rest, eating less, and studying more. Only the Sabbath had the power to draw him away from his books. Dov Baer worked his way through the Talmud, its commentaries, and the Torah. Finally, Lemberg had no more to offer him but reverence. He returned home and dutifully accepted in marriage the woman his family had selected for him.

It is hard to imagine what his parents had been thinking of; the bride was a financial disaster. She offered her husband impeccable ancestry and character—nothing more. Perhaps there was a close friendship between the two families or possibly the bride had spiritual qualities that were considered essentially appropriate for such a scholar. It may have been that Dov Baer's father was the kind of tenderhearted man who always comes off second best in a bargain. Or perhaps both fathers anticipated that the precocious young scholar would soon be making enough money as an important rabbi to support not only his young wife but both families as well. If that expectation had loomed large in their plans, they were in for a nasty shock.

Dov Baer refused to become a rabbi. He told his dismayed family that the Torah should be an object of study and veneration, not a tool in a trade. Since he had no trade, he became a teacher. And in those days teachers were very poor. The early years of Dov Baer's marriage were an anguish. Though he had been poor as a child, he had also been much admired and looked upon with hope. In childhood, confidence had surged through him. As a husband and then a father, he found himself unable to provide his family with enough to nourish them adequately, far less to provide them with simple dignity. He had disappointed his family and all the villagers. He had not even made himself happy. He loved children and delighted in watching and helping them learn, but he felt unfulfilled in his work. He was floundering, uncertain how to satisfy himself and his obligations at the same time.

After a time he turned back to the holy books that had seemed in childhood to be the key to his future. He began exploring the books of the Kabbalah, finding Isaac Luria's commentaries most stirring. With resoluteness that was typical of him, he flung himself into the austerities Luria recommended as the most effective method of acquiring mystical knowledge.

Humility had never been and would never be one of his virtues. But in his plunge into exercises to weaken the flesh, Dov Baer would have done well to have congratulated himself on having already been an ascetic. All his life he had gone without proper sleep, eaten only as much as absolutely necessary, and deprived himself of normal recreation. He had driven his body beyond its limits. As he began driving it harder, nourishing it less, his body broke down. He became sick, unable to teach. Without the little his teaching brought in, his family had no money for food.

As soon as his health permitted, Dov Baer compromised to the extent of becoming a *maggid*, an itinerant preacher who taught about God by stories and homilies. His preaching reached not only the villagers who came to hear him but a personality inside himself which had remained hidden within the timid aspect of the scholar. He was a lion among the maggidim. His words throbbed with emotion. He could capture his audience with a story, a parable, a joke, and hold them hushed and taut for hours. Not only peasants, but scholars came to listen to him, impressed by the depth of his learning and caught up in the passion of his feeling. There were many wandering preachers in those days, but Dov Baer became *the* Maggid; and the towns of Korets and Dubno invited him to take permanent positions there.

Characteristically, he threw too much of himself into the effort. He spoke for two and three hours and when his listeners wanted more, he went on for an added bit, even though he was spent and trembling. Never having completely abandoned them, he had taken up his Lurianic disciplines again to give his sermons added authority. Soon history repeated itself. His meager physical reserves were soon spent and his health began to crumble.

Frightened, his family tried to persuade the Maggid to go for help to the healer whose miracles were being talked about from village to village. Dov Baer shook his head, believing that miracles were the property of God. Further, he had heard about Israel Baal Shem Tov from scholars. He was not impressed.

Perversely his physical condition worsened. Finally he

could endure the pain and the nagging no longer. He agreed to go to Medziboz. There, instead of a paragon, he found an uncouth old man dressed like a peasant and, like a peasant, given to smoking a pipe and gossiping about village matters. Disgusted and blaming himself for giving in to nonsense, the Maggid returned to his room determined to give up his fool's errand and return home in the morning. He was preparing for bed when the messenger came requesting the meeting that changed his life.

It may have saved it as well—at least for a few important years. Overwhelmed by the Besht's holiness and mysticism, Dov Baer yielded to his revulsion for asceticism. For his part the Besht was not content with endowing his new disciple with the spiritual and occult fruits of a lifetime's work. Although he was only ten years older than Dov Baer, he took him into his household and watched over his physical welfare with the tender concern of a father.

What the Maggid felt for the Besht is more difficult to determine. He soaked up his training in occultism and mysticism; it has even been said that he learned from the Besht the language of plants and animals. There is no question that his religious thought was more strongly influenced by his teacher than by any other source. Dov Baer's torah as it comes down transcribed by his disciple, Solomon of Lutsk, testifies to that. Nevertheless, following the Besht's death there was none of Jacob Joseph's reiteration of "my master" in the Maggid's speech. He spoke of himself and his methods until many wondered if indeed he still considered himself the Besht's disciple or was attempting to found a new school of his own. Once he had obtained the majority of the Hasidim's consent to be their zaddik—Phenehus of Korets, for one, never recognized him—he required that the Hasid headquarters be relocated in his own town where people were accustomed to think of him as the holy man; he would not move his family to the town that was his master's shrine. Such outward gestures would have meant little to the Besht himself. What would have concerned him were changes in the emotional and intellectual components of Hasidism that the Maggid brought about.

The Besht had brought his intimate disciples into his own family. The result was a household that was much like that of any peasant living with his grown sons, only larger and more gleeful.

Dov Baer converted that simple, comfortable household into a formal court that he dominated like a prince. Instead of living among his disciples family style, he made grand entrances, an image in white—the color of light radiating from the Kabbalist's first two Sefirot—from his white satin robes to his white shoes and white snuff box. And he moved through the court like a stagy performer of the mystic, pressing long thin hands to his forehead in theatrical silence during the communal third meal on the Sabbath while his disciples watched in wonder and tried to swallow a few morsels of food down emotion-choked throats.

And when the Maggid did speak, it was in aphorisms and sermons. There was little of the personal inquiry about health and family. And there was none of the boisterous joking and buffoonery between him and his disciples.

Part of the display, of course, was only a reflection of the inevitable differences in personality between two men. And part of it was the Maggid's wretched health that plagued him more and more as age added its own complications. He did not like, and his body could not tolerate, shoulder-rubbing intimacy. But the expense he poured into the court's accommodations and his own dress, the customs ritualized into ceremony, the attitudes of awe and worship, his policy of sealing himself off from his followers—these were not inevitable. One cannot help thinking that the Besht could not have felt comfortable in the ritualistic elegance of the Maggid's court. And what would he have thought of its costly and lavish appointments? Once, after the Besht and his son Zevi had visited the home of a rich man, Israel had remarked sympathetically that he knew his son envied the man's beautiful possessions but if they belonged to him, he would sell them and give them to the poor. Certainly, in later days the Besht's poverty was a matter of choice. He could have lived in luxury if he had kept for himself all the money that he gave to the poor.

In addition to altering the life-style of the Hasidic zaddik—an alteration that was to become permanent—the Maggid interjected a complex speculative system into Hasidic thought which could only result in introducing elements of scholasticism and intellectual theorizing into the Hasidic method.

Although the Besht had used some Lurianic terminology and borrowed some of its liturgy and concepts, he did not permit his being to stray from the state of devekut to abstruse philosophizing. For the Besht, the Shekhinah was God as He can be experienced on earth. A survey of his teachings as they have come down to us through his disciples leads to the conclusion that he did not concern himself with abstract distinctions between God, his Shekhinah, and the *Ein Soph* as the Kabbalists do.

It seems likely that as his mystical powers developed, the Besht did not use terminology, concentrating his attention on achieving his goal instead. We know he had visions of the prophets. We know he had at least one vision of the Messiah. What form—if form is the proper word—his other visions took is not known. But one point is certain: when the Besht urged the achievement of devekut, he was stressing adherence to rather than specific details about different spheres of divinity. Possibly he knew that the object of devekut could not be contained by language. The writings of his disciple Jacob Joseph show a similar lack of concern for intellectual theorizing; they focus attention on method.

It was not so with Dov Baer. He became a mystic, but he never lost his passion for philosophic speculation. To him devekut carried more of the Kabbalistic connotation of a mystical ladder or series of levels of attainment than the simple state of fixing one's being on God. The Maggid speculated that when the ordinary worshipper finally achieved devekut, he was clinging to the Shekhinah, which according to Kabbalistic reckoning is the lowest of the ten Sefirot or spheres of divinity and the feminine aspect of the divine world. However, through devekut, the possibility of being able to reach higher and higher Sefirot exists. Dov Baer let it be known among his disciples that when he meditated he was clinging to the Sefirot of *hokhman* (wisdom) or *ayin* (the nothingness that precedes creation), that is to say the two highest Sefirot. (See *Understanding the Kabbalah*, Edward Albertson. Los Angeles, California 1972.)

Many religious theoreticians believe such a devekut impossible due to the indescribable energy of the higher Sefirot. They speculate that a separation between man and the higher Sefirot will exist until the world as we know it comes to an end and the souls of men are no longer contaminated by evil.

Dov Baer pictured the existence of mankind as a decline from a previous state, a decline that had a purpose. When God created the universe, a disunity came about. This disunity desires to be healed. Man's soul descends to the material plane, and by means of its spiritual exaltation, raises the material existence toward a reunion with divinity. Man's reason for being is to renounce concrete reality and return to the mystical nothingness that preceded creation (ayin). It is impossible, the Maggid theorized, for anything to pass from one existence to another without becoming nothing at the point of transition. God created existence out of nothing (ayin) and He makes nothingness (ayin) out of existence.

Dov Baer included in his speculative organization the concept of *zimzum*. But Dov Baer's concept differed from the one that Isaac Luria originally put forth. Isaac Luria conceived of zimzum as a contraction. For Dov Baer, zimzum was a form of comprehension which acts mystically to compel God to appear according to the laws of the intellect. Dov Baer interpreted the verse in Song 7:6: "The king is held captive in the tresses" to mean that God is held captive in the logic of the mind. For this reason Dov Baer dismissed the value of supplication in prayer. And, unlike the Besht and Jacob Joseph, he himself did not feel drawn to send torrents of praise to God. For the Maggid, prayer was a mystical tool, a psychological exercise. He thought of it almost as an occult ritual that produced in the same mechanistic style of all occult rituals invariable results.

Such concepts are pretty heavy going for a tired peasant or a villager with no more schooling behind him than that obtained in a cramped, one-room school presided over by a poor man, harassed by his own personal problems and over-awed by the community's prominent citizens. In fact, Dov Baer's combination of Aristotelian and Kabbalistic theory and theosophic language is difficult even for scholars trained in abstruse progressions of thought, and it was such men as these who became his favorite audience.

Despite his vanity, he cannot be written off as a man who failed his teacher. The Maggid was a complex man and a man of contradictions. Physically, though tall, he was frail and crippled, with an invalid's pallor. But he had the will power of a bulldozer. His court throbbed with activity. He managed his disciples like a high-powered top executive of an international corporation. His emissaries spread out across eastern Europe, con-verting, setting up conventicles, intervening in social prob-lems and political issues. He had scholars working under him to effect changes in and simplify religious law. He introduced changes in the tradition of butchering meat. The minutiae of everyday life and details of procedure were as important to him as celestial theory.

For the Besht and Jacob Joseph the Hasids were a mystical brotherhood of saints and would-be saints. Under the Maggid the brotherhood became a clearly defined move-ment, an organization that was as visible from the outside as from the inside. He supervised everything. And though he was too sick to travel, his presence drew streams of fiery young enthusiasts to his court for him to teach and to dazzle.

Men came to him to be dazzled. One of his disciples boasted that he had traveled to the Maggid not to hear him teach but to watch him lace up his boots. Dov Baer encouraged worship and he became the object of worship. His followers whispered together about the meaning of his smallest gestures. Everything he did, the nuances of his tone and glance, symbolized texts of mystical lore. He told his disciples that God had given him, as zaddik, dominion over the physical and spiritual world. The zaddik was the reflection of God on earth. God revealed Himself to the community through the zaddik and through the zaddik bestowed His mercy and grace upon the community. It was the community's duty to obey the zaddik and to give to him gifts of time and money.

Nevertheless, vain as he was, proud as he was, this man of contrasts was one of the few disciples of the Baal Shem Tov to reject completely spiritual elitism. He taught that every man is capable of becoming a zaddik. Not birthright but meditation and prayer determined spiritual success. It does not seem likely that he felt that the divine emanation, or, to put it in Lurianic terms, the number of divine sparks, in each man was equal; he did believe that each man possessed the necessary qualifications to achieve devekut with the two highest Sefirot during his lifetime—provided, of course, that he was willing to devote sufficient time and energy to his mystical efforts. Redemption, he told his disciples, had ceased to be a single historical event and had become a continuous spiritual experience for the individual.

Further, and more extraordinary in terms of his personality, he made the point that although the zaddik's chief function was to use his own mystical powers to help his followers achieve their spiritual goals, spiritual success was not dependent upon finding a zaddik. Effort and practice, Dov Baer stressed again and again, were the most important elements in mysticism.

Although Dov Baer regarded prayer as a tool, he taught

that a potent part of that tool was a solid structure of inward emotion. Mere mouthing of words would accomplish nothing. He was fond of saying that the words of the Torah possessed matter as well as spirit and those worshippers who studied its words with a cold heart were not in contact with its spirit. When prayer is transferred from the lips to thought, the human act is converted into divine speech.

He despised hypocrites who wrapped themselves in their prayer shawls and bound their arms and foreheads with phylacteries, but failed to put their hearts into their prayers. Those exercises that encourage piety were to him the most important part of a man's religious life. The Maggid stressed the effectiveness of meditation. Extending the Lurianic doctrine of zimzum to the individual, he told his disciples that just as God concentrated Himself during the act of creation in order to make "room" for the finite world, so the worshipper can concentrate his thought on God as a focal point so that his soul becomes attached to God. By this type of concentration man can break through the corruption of everyday life and conquer the very laws of Nature.

The whole earth, the Maggid preached, is in the Holy One. It is the world that stands in God, not God in the world.

On this point, he was every bit his master's disciple, and like the Besht, he inferred from this principle that physical acts such as eating and drinking and sensual experiences can further spiritual life. Man can worship through corporality, he taught, and he can achieve devekut through the performance of physical acts.

This concept is a daring one that has been espoused across time and space by true mystics—men whose spiritual yearnings are the strongest pull in their lives. They can participate in and enjoy the sensuous aspects of life, even derive from them the strength of renewal and re-creation without being in the least tempted by pleasures to give up their primary goal. For them nothing is as compelling, as exciting, as stimulating, as maddeningly, tauntingly desirable as the next "bend" in their spiritual adventures.

Those with less strong spiritual drives view this concept with horror. For them sensuous experience presents a terrible, frightening temptation. For them the pleasures of the world are so much keener, so much more compelling than their fragile desire to seek God that continually worldly pleasures threaten to overwhelm and destroy their desire for God. These men can protect and nurture their spiritual aspirations only by isolating them from temptation.

For a man with Dov Baer's ambitions and vanity to uphold such a doctrine was more than daring, it was heroic. Sensuous experience was looked upon with grave suspicion in the world in which he moved, and for a religious man to propose that physical pleasures could be put to spiritual uses was in itself a scandal. The brotherhood was hated and under attack by the established orthodoxy for no better reasons than jealousy and greed in far too many cases. Jealousy and greed, though excellent motivating forces, make a poorer platform for opposition than prurience and wantonness. By continuing to teach his master's method of spiritualizing the physical aspects of life rather than attempting to suppress them, Dov Baer was risking his desire for an empire.

Daring and stubbornness were just as much a part of Dov Baer's character as vanity. His own experiences had taught him that the Besht's method was more effective than the repression that had gripped the religious life of his people. For all his love of display, an empty empire was not worth the struggle. Like the Besht, he was fighting for an empire of new spirituality. That could not be built on fear or prejudice. He had ruined his health and risked his life experimenting with mystical exercise. Now he was risking his empire to give to his students the benefits of his learning.

The Maggid was aware, however, that the physical world did act on some more cruelly than on others. He acknowledged that the worship of God through the senses was not a discipline for everyone, just as he pointed out that some zaddikim need to remove themselves from social contact while others are able to continue their spiritual exploration and take an active part in community affairs. He was not trying to force everyone to walk in his footsteps; he was working for freedom for the various personality types to find the way most suited to them.

In applying the concept that the world stands within God, the Maggid rejected Lurianic dualism that stresses the extremes of good and evil. As a prophylactic against the negative side of this dualism, Isaac Luria had advocated and devised extreme forms of physical penance. These measures had captured the imagination of many of the more devout members of the eastern European community. As in the case of the Maggid, more often than not, the captured imagination was forerunner to ruined health. Unfortunately, the emotional trauma of pessimism and distrust was even more damaging than the physical effects. With the highest motives and the best of intentions scores of people were making their lives and those of people around them into a hell on earth.

Dov Baer's main purpose in opposing Lurianic dualism was not hygienic, however. He was trying to open the minds of those around him to a higher reality. He had reached a vista in his mystical experience that allowed him to see mankind and to see creation not as a battleground over which good and evil forces contested but as part of God's holy presence. The vista had changed his life, making it rich and meaningful rather than bleak and frightening. In opposing this concept of Luria, whom he admired, he was telling his disciples, "This is what I've seen. Look and you can see it too."

Nevertheless, once again the orthodox community was shocked. Only a devil would suggest that evil was relative. And when the Maggid asserted that even heathen idols contained sparks of the divine Shekhinah, they shook their heads in horror. But out of every hundred enemies he made, there would be one person who listened and did not shake his head, who began to see God in his world instead of demons.

Mysticism, philosophy, organization, vanity, and courage—these were the five characteristics the Maggid brought to his leadership of the Hasidic movement. Each left an indelible mark upon the brotherhood. Dov Baer had substantially changed the characteristics of the brotherhood, but it is possible that without some of those changes, the brotherhood would not have survived. Certainly, it prospered and expanded under his leadership. Ironically, its successful expansion may have been indirectly responsible for hastening his death.

The rapid proliferation of Hasidic conventicles encouraged the Maggid to send emissaries northward across the Polish border into Lithuania. There the Hasidic movement struck a headland of conservatism and almost sank. The headland was Elijah of Wilna, Elijah Gaon, the Great. The great Elijah had no official standing in the community. He had always shunned public office. But to Jews from Europe to the Holy Land, he was orthodox Judaism at its finest. He had been a precocious child, a brilliant scholar, and in his maturity he was, if not mystical, pious and saintly.

Elijah the Great was not, however, a flexible individual. He knew of only one path to heaven, and as far as he was concerned, all other paths led to hell. He was not a litigious man. He kept out of the squabbles that so many of his contemporaries spent their lives on. But he was a man of duty and his duty was to the religious authority that from ancient times had linked his people to God.

Modest he was, but he was also aware that in Lithuania and beyond, the Jewish community looked to him as an example. His actions and his attitudes would be imitated across the face of Europe.

In 1772· this exemplar of orthodoxy discovered, almost under his doorstep, the presence of a secret Hasid conventicle—praying noisily and grotesquely, preaching the equality of good and evil, encouraging sensual depravity, luring the young away from their books and fasts—a veritable spore of the Evil One. He swooped down on the new sect like an avenging angel, ordered its members whipped, and issued a public declaration repudiating Hasidism, declaring, among other points, "If I had the power, I would have punished the infidels as the worshippers of Baal were punished of old."

Despite the oblique threat of stoning, if this incident had occurred during the lifetime of the Besht, the storm would have spent itself breaking over his unresponsive head. His own humility was an effective buffer against the sting of attack. His faith convinced him that the future would vindicate his cause. He did such work as found acceptance and, for the rest, he was more likely to be amused than consternated by the uproar of his opponents.

The Maggid had no such insulation. Vanity was his great weakness and the blow struck at a time when his body was once again paying the price of his earlier immodest excesses of asceticism. Within the year—December 15, 1772—he was dead.

His vanity may have killed him, but it did not destroy his work. His disciples were an extraordinary band of men— extraordinary in their holiness, extraordinary in their individualism, and extraordinary in their energy. He had made them so.

5

Excommunication

THE COMBINED EFFECTS of the Maggid's death and Elijah the Great's edict were catastrophic. Grief, panic, fury, and bewilderment swept through the Hasidic conventicles. No one knew what to do. Dov Baer had trained his disciples to be assistants, not to take command of the sprawling organization.

Leadership was what the Hasidim desperately needed at the moment. Many of the brothers felt that Rabbi Shneur Zalman of Ladi was the best man to assume Dov Baer's authority. Piety, character, scholarship, brilliance—all these he had, but nevertheless, Shneur Zalman was widely disliked among the Hasidim.

He was a Litvach for one thing, and in those days national antagonism was considered a virtue. For another, Rabbi Zalman was a late comer to the Maggid's court, an upstart, many of the Maggid's disciples felt. During the time he had been a disciple, Dov Baer had kept him so busy that he never had the time to become friendly with the others. Perhaps without meaning to, Dov Baer had made the others' jealousy worse by praising his new disciple too lavishly and holding him up as an example to the rest of them.

Perceiving the resentment, Shneur Zalman refused the leadership, suggesting instead that it be given to Rabbi Menahem Mendel of Permyshlany, a disciple of the Besht's. The others agreed with relief.

Rabbi Menahem Mendel had all the spiritual qualities one would expect in a zaddik. He was an ardent enthusiast of the Besht's teaching. He believed that devotion was the pivot of a man's life. His own devotion to God shone in everything he did. Antischolastic all his life, not only did he feel that studying the Torah was not necessary to obtain devekut, but he took the firm position that it was a detriment, distracting the worshipper from his spiritual exercises. Prayer and meditation on the greatness of the Creator—this was the fastest and safest path to redemption. Like his master and Dov Baer, he was above the duality of good and evil. He told his followers not to become melancholy over past sins, but to go forward in confidence.

This point of view rocked the sin-sensitive Polish rabbinate on its heels. Here was another threat to the moral fiber of the community: another Hasidic zaddik who scorned study of the Torah, and penance, and was openly casual about sin.

Rabbi Menahem Mendel, like the Besht, was untroubled by the scurrilous tongues of foolish men. His attention was focused on his plans to take up residence in the Holy Land. There was nothing of the organizer or empire-builder about him. He assumed the brotherhood would take care of itself as it had in the days of his master.

However, it was a different brotherhood by this time with different needs, and Shneur Zalman was keenly aware of those needs. A scholar, he stood more in awe of the intellectual rabbinate than did Rabbi Menahem Mendel. He knew the temper of the young Hasidim as well. Sincerity and eagerness they had, but most of them were not noted for their meekness. Shneur Zalman feared that, with no one to guide them, their fury at being banned would explode into action that would further provoke the community and widen the breach between the brotherhood and the orthodox religious leadership.

His efforts to find the most effective and least damaging response to Elijah the Great's edict gradually involved Shneur Zalman in directing the brotherhood's activities. Of course, he did nothing without consulting Rabbi Menahem Mendel, who was delighted to be shed of the chore. The difficulty with this arrangement was that, since he had no formal authority, headstrong conventicle leaders felt free to follow their own judgment whenever they wished.

For all its heavy ritual and conservatism, there have always been in Jewish religious life deep currents of individualism and personal independence. As a rebel organization, the brotherhood had attracted men whose personalities were strongly dominated by these characteristics. To hold the brotherhood on a single course had taken the charismatic qualities of leaders like the Besht and the Maggid. For all their greatness neither Rabbi Menahem Mendel nor Shneur Zalman was charismatic. In retrospect, this combination of factors has certain elements of comic opera. At the time, the principals from either side thought it was anything but funny. In part the humor comes from changes in attitude. On the contemporary scene, religious issues do not loom with the overweaning importance they did then. It is difficult for us today to see what all the fuss was about, but in the eighteenth century, men *knew* they were engaged in a struggle for men's souls. And the stakes were higher than individual souls. If the community permitted an outrage to the eyes of the Lord to spawn unchallenged in its midst, the coming of the Messiah was endangered. Not surprisingly, emotion spilled over from the religious leaders to the most secular member of the community. The times were tense. Pent-up anguish needed an outlet. Desire to strike a blow against the Galuth was strong in people whose everyday lives were a disaster. Since both sides of the combat believed that they were hastening the coming of the Messiah and the other side was threatening it, it was not how the battle was fought but the winning that seemed important.

Had Shneur Zalman possessed the power to control the Hasidim, the crisis would have passed with little more harm done than a temporary respite in the movement's growth. Rabbi Zalman had an old head on his young shoulders and a heart respectful of good even in the bosom of his opponents. As it was, he tried valiantly. Feeling certain that, given the opportunity, he could convince Elijah the Great of the worthiness of the Hasidic movement, his first attempt was a journey to Elijah's city. Wilna, the capital of Lithuania, was famous throughout Europe as the center of the highest type of rabbinical scholasticism. Often termed with honor the Jerusalem of Lithuania, it had become a city of pilgrimage.

It was a tense pilgrimage for young Shneur Zalman, journeying with saintly, frail Rabbi Menahem Mendel by his side, hoping to arrange a formal debate and convince the most redoubtable figure in European Jewish orthodoxy. As it happened, he had girded himself for nothing. Elijah—his eyes on the Torah's admonishment to refrain from looking an evil man in the face—had slipped out of the city, refusing to return until the infidels had left.

The young Hasidim went wild with disappointment and rage, crying out that Elijah was afraid to debate with Shneur Zalman. Shneur Zalman was disappointed but not bitter. He urged his brothers by word and letter not to speak or even think disrespectfully of Elijah the Great. But his words met only impatient shakings of the head and mutterings.

Again, later, when the head of the synagogue that Elijah attended formally burned a copy of Jacob Joseph's newly published book on the synagogue's steps—the Hasidim howled, swearing vengeance and ignoring impatiently Shneur Zalman's letters pleading for tolerance and suggesting Elijah knew nothing of the insult.

Had the young Hasidic brothers cowered and repentantly modified their more obvious customs, the furor might have died down and people's attention might have returned to the task of staying alive; but the brothers' praying was as noisy and extravagantly physical as ever. In the Hasid headquarters there was dancing and singing and shouts of joy—and shouts of defiance, unseemly challenges to the person of Elijah the Great, and even insults.

The community's wrath grew. Hasidism was a menace and must be stamped out.

Although not enjoying political or legal power within their host nations, European Jewish communities were able to exert a wide range of pressures on one of their own who incurred their censure. Outright physical violence was not unknown; the police rarely bothered themselves with disturbances in the ghetto unless the outbreak threatened to disturb the peace or offend the sensibilities of the Christians. And a Jew in fear of bodily harm had no reason to regard the police as protectors. More usual and more effective in the long run was a kind of absolute exclusion the community could inflict upon the individual and his family. No one would talk to or deal with those under the ban. If the banned were merchants or craftsmen, no one would buy their goods. They could not buy food in the marketplace. There would be no midwife for the woman in labor, no healer for the feverish child. A healthy child would not be admitted into the heder, nor could he find friends to play with. And who would marry the children when they grew older? Of course, the synagogue would be closed to them. And in the most tragic cases, even death did not stop their troubles, for their corpses could not be buried in the consecrated graveyard.

Even if there was no formal ban, in a small town or village, suspicion and disapproval made themselves felt in very painful ways.

The Hasidic families had been enduring distrust for years. Elijah the Great's ban had deepened and quickened resentment against them, forcing many Hasidim who lived in largely orthodox villages and towns to resort to the self-betrayal of publicly practicing conventions they felt were decadent while secretly continuing their joyous worship of the wonders of God. It was hard enough for the farmers, the craftsmen, and the small merchants to dissemble, but those who suffered the most emotionally and materialistically were the rabbis who had converted to Hasidism.

Rabbis were considered leaders of the community. In another sense they were more dependent upon the community than the peasants. They were the scholars, but their education was narrow. In truth a man who had given his boyhood to God and the Torah was too ignorant to follow any profession but religion. Farmers and merchants did not think of themselves as educated because they acquired their skills gradually while doing chores for their fathers. Nevertheless, a man coming to their trades without such an apprenticeship were almost certain to fail.

A scholar was fitted for nothing except to teach or preach or heal or, if he wished to live the most comfortably, to be a rabbi. And any of these professions involved direct community support. The custom of marrying a scholar young increased his financial dependency and inflicted him with two sets of parents to care for and be scolded by. Even when his wife's family was wealthy, the young scholar's financial dilemma was by no means eased. The chances were that his father-in-law had arranged the match to acquire a hotshot provider not a mystic. Unless he behaved as his father-in-law wished, the scholar was likely to lose all annuities and his wife as well. Or what was from a realistic standpoint worse, not to lose his wife and be forced to support her and the babies as they came along. In his early manhood a scholar was more like a valuable commodity to be used by the real powers in the community than a man with resources and position of his own.

Jacob Joseph had been caught up and whirled about by the force of these social realities. They were also to engulf the lives of Levi Yitzhok and his family. Levi Yitzhok was already a married man, although still a student, when he first heard Samuel Horowitz tell about the mystical knowledge that could be acquired by the Hasidic method. It took a hunger strike to obtain his father-in-law's permission to take up residence in Riczivol so that he might study under Samuel Horowitz. His curiosity and dissatisfaction with the life he knew drove him on. And Samuel Horowitz led him to Dov Baer.

From the moment of that meeting, his father-in-law's plans were doomed. Levi Yitzhok refused to return home and took up residence in the Maggid's court. Quickly he became the living fulfillment of the Maggid's requirements in a disciple. He followed Dov Baer around like a shadow and few of his words escaped Levi Yitzhok's furiously scribbling pen. His master's least gesture had religious significance for him.

Left to himself, he would have served Dov Baer until the Maggid's death. However, disaster struck his father-in-law's business and his health did not permit him to start in again supporting the family. Unless Levi Yitzhok was willing to allow his family to starve, he had to find a rabbinate for himself.

His former teacher Samuel Horowitz left Riczivol and it seemed natural to the congregation to offer the vacant position to his student Levi. Levi's reluctance to accept was nothing compared to that of his congregation when they learned that he had changed from a nice orthodox scholar to an impassioned Hasid.

Samuel Horowitz had been able to keep his Hasidic leanings locked up inside, unless and until he happened on a likely prospect for conversion. His ability to be discreet had accomplished much good and there is no doubt about Levi's admiration for his former teacher, but he was made of different stuff. Compromise and pretense were impossible for Levi. He talked as he thought and lived as he felt, with short regard for consequences. The consequences fell hard and soon enough, and Levi Yitzhok found himself without salary or synagogue. He tried taking over a synagogue in Pinsk, thinking that the suburb of the Hasid-dominated city of Karlin would be lenient to his views. For a year his anticipations were justified. People listened to him if not always with pleasure at least with tolerance. Then news of Elijah the Great's ban hit the suburb. Proud of its tradition of scholarship, Pinsk's more orthodox factions' resistance to Hasidism crystallized and broke into angry opposition. Levi Yitzhok watched in horror as his congregation became a ferment of hot words and conflict. Finally, to stop the wrangling, he fled once again.

Horror, grief, hunger he knew. But he also knew prayer. And for him prayer had become a self-forgetting ecstasy. There are two kinds of saintliness: one that battles and conquers evil, and the other that neither battles nor encounters nor recognizes it, existing in a holy state beyond evil. Such an innocent was Levi Yitzhok. He loved God and he loved God's people, and he could no more believe there was evil in God's people than he could believe there was evil in God Himself.

He refused to believe the teaching that Jews suffered as a punishment for disobeying God's commandments. His defense of the Jews went farther than expostulating with sin-obsessed rabbis. The legends of his daring defense of them before the throne of God are still being told in the hamlets and villages of Europe. When Levi Yitzhok came upon a family who were poor or had suffered at the hands of the Christians, he would cry out angrily to God that the Jews suffered for His sake. Because of their adherence to God they were regarded by their enemies as sheep for slaughter. Often during holy services, he was known to burst out in an impromptu petition on behalf of the Jews. Once on Yom Kippur he went so far as, publicly during prayer, to summon the God of Justice to trial on behalf of his client the people of Israel.

Despite his own persecution at their hands, to this defender the people of Israel were a constant wonder and delight. One time when a young man from his congregation failed to keep one of the ritual fasts, Levi Yitzhok asked him hopefully if he had forgotten what day it was. The young man, angry and defiant, told him no and again no to the suggestion that sickness had prevented him from fasting. Looking toward heaven triumphantly, Levi Yitzhok cried out, "Lord, what a truthful people the Jews are!"

Because poverty kept so many of the peasants from taking the time to learn Hebrew, most of his prayers and torah were in Yiddish. One of his Yiddish prayers, *The Kaddish of Levi Yitzhok*, has been preserved as have been many of his sermons.

It was not until he was forty-five that Levi Yitzhok finally found a town that would give back the love he offered. It was the city of Berdichev, and no mean refuge, but a city whose

Jewish tradition went back four hundred years and which was considered the most important center of Judaism in Volhynia.

From the beginning Berditchev perceived the holiness of its new rabbi and flourished in his care and listened to his teachings. Self-forgetful as he was in prayer, he never forgot community affairs, instructing his disciples to interrupt him—even if he was studying the Torah—when the city council was to discuss a new community ordinance, so that he might hurry to watch over the interests of those in his trust.

He regarded all the poor as his special province. When the council, feeling the pinch of a bad year, was debating a regulation that would prohibit beggars who were not citizens from entering the city, he scolded them all soundly. When the peasants came to town for one of their rare visits to the synagogue, they found that the rabbi of Berditchev deferred to them and escorted them to the front of the synagogue as though they were wealthy merchants. On one occasion, it is said, he kept the congregation waiting while one farmer recited the alphabet in lieu of the ritual prayer he never had time to learn. And frequently, rather than have the town's tailor miss a single word of the service, he delayed it until the tailor could close up his shop and reach the temple.

In the latter part of his life, disciples literally forced themselves on Levi Yitzhok. He taught them with gentle words and example, losing his temper only when he came upon cruelty and exploitation. The man who for forty-five years could not find a place for himself and his family became one of the prime forces in spreading Hasidism into Lithuania and the Ukraine and the most loved man in Berdichev.

6

The Charade, Chains
and Two Czars

TIME DID NOT soften Elijah the Great's attitude about the new sect, but he was a scholar and a gentle man. Having made his position clear on the subject, he had turned his attention to more congenial matters.

Almost a quarter of a century went by. Community antagonism had quieted down. Once again the Hasidim were becoming more visible and were expanding.

Then some firebrand with a flair for the theater decided he could completely nullify the effects of Elijah the Great's ban. He organized a skit that could have been billed as The Banishment of Elijah's Son and in 1796 sent it to play the great commercial cities of Germany.

The skit had a dramatis personae of two: the son of Elijah the Great and attendant. The attendant had all the lines. The script called for him in the course of their travels to let it slip that his silent master was none other than the son of the great Elijah of Wilna. The son was performing for his father the penance of exile in order to achieve atonement for his father's persecution of the Hasidim. In answer to the inevitable questions, the attendant went on to explain that time had given Elijah the wisdom to perceive the holy nature of the Hasidic movement and now he wished with all his heart that more Jews would listen to its teachings and follow its ways.

For a time the ruse worked. Propitious rumors rippled back from Germany and the conventicles enjoyed new prestige and a surge of interest. Inevitably news of the "penance" reached the attention of Elijah the Great. He was a man of many characteristics, but humor was not among them. His temper surged in a volcanic explosion that was felt throughout the Judaic world. On June 22, 1796, he denied the false penance and excommunicated the Hasidic movement in the stern, relentless language of the ancient prophets, calling for a complete ostracism of all who dabbled with the diabolic sect.

In a day the Hasidim had lost the work of twenty-five years; they were worse off than they had been after the first, milder ban. Some of the conventicle leaders panicked before the catastrophe, spreading rumors to the effect that Elijah had issued no second ban, that the story was a lie, that the good Elijah had said no word against the Hasidim.

Communication being what it was then, contradictory stories—charges and counter-charges—bewildered the entire European Jewish community. No one knew what to believe or discredit. On October 14, 1796, Elijah of Wilna formally put an end to the confusion by issuing a proclamation to be read to the Jewish communities of Lithuania, White Russia, Volhynia, and Podolsk, containing these words:

> Woe unto this generation. They [the Hasidim] violate the Law, distort our teachings, and set up a new covenant. They lay snares in the house of the Lord; it behooves us to punish these madmen before the whole world for their own improvement. Let none have pity on them and grant them shelter.

This letter was read aloud in the synagogues and other public assemblies and posted in the marketplace and other locations where it would likely be read. It was a stunning attack. The enemies of Hasidism believed it a killing one, and the Hasidim for a time were not certain that they were in error.

Less than a year after making his proclamation Elijah the Great was dead.

The Hasidim behaved with characteristic abandon. At the news, they danced in the streets, shouting for joy and singing praise to God.

Wilna was outraged. The community leaders organized a committee to keep the doings of the Hasidim under surveillance and to punish them whenever their behavior wavered from orthodox standards. Given time to take its full effect, this action might have been fatal. Certainly the Hasidim stood shamed and disgraced in the eyes of the community. Few wanted to associate with them and fewer still were willing to take the risks of doing so.

However, among Elijah the Great's following there were hotheads also. They were fuming over the insult to their leader, muttering among themselves that a stronger punishment was due the Hasidim. With the talking, their anger grew and strategies and counter-strategies were formed. Finally, one of them, a rabbi named Avigdor, fused the emotion into action. He went to the police and accused Shneur Zalman of disloyalty to the Russian sovereign. As a result Shneur Zalman and twenty-two brother Hasidim were arrested and imprisoned.

The Jewish community was horrified. Avigdor had broken the unwritten law that the community copes with its own problems, never giving their hated rulers an opportunity to meddle in Jewish affairs. Disgust at Rabbi Avigdor's act and sympathy for any Jew thrown in a czarist prison neutralized much of the hatred against the Hasidim. The charge was so obviously false that the government soon released all the prisoners except Shneur Zalman. He was sent to St. Petersburg in chains.

The event was marvelous publicity for the Hasidic cause. But at the time the brotherhood was too terrified at the prospects of losing their ex-officio leader to enjoy its effect. The Russian government was not noted for its justice even to Christians. A Jew's best chance in the czar's courts was bribery.

Quickly, the brotherhood gathered together 60,000 rubles—considering the straits they were in that was squeezing blood out of a turnip—and sent it through the proper channels. Shneur Zalman wrote his own defense in Hebrew—his Russian was not up to the occasion—and had it translated into the language of the land. The defense was presented to the minister of justice and must have impressed him. On November 15, 1798, Shneur Zalman was released from prison on order from Czar Paul I.

The episode made Shneur Zalman a hero among his own. That day, the day of his release, was proclaimed a day of celebration within the brotherhood.

If anything, the ordeal had deepened the piety of Shneur Zalman. He had been chanting the verse from the psalm, "He redeemed my soul in peace," when the news of his release came. And his response to the praise of his Hasidic brothers was to use their new-found admiration of him for the purpose of building harmony between the brotherhood and the community. He begged his brothers to moderate their anger, repeating again and again his conviction that Elijah would not have tolerated such behavior from his followers, were he alive to prevent it.

On the other hand the episode with its sequel increased the rage and vindictiveness of Rabbi Avigdor. This time he prepared a lengthy petition to Czar Paul I, accusing Shneur Zalman of preaching that allegiance to God requires man to disregard his temporal rulers, and specifically linking him to the openly seditious Sabbathian movement, claiming the Hasidic brotherhood was sending large sums of money to Palestine to be used for purposes against the interests of the Russian throne.

Once again Shneur Zalman found himself on the way to St. Petersburg in chains. This time he was imprisoned in the fortress of St. Peter and Paul, a "maximum security" fortress reserved for dangerous persons, and for prisoners a very dismal hole.

Incredibly, Shneur Zalman was able once again to impress the czarist government with his innocence. Three weeks after walking into the dungeon, he was released on condition that he remain in St. Petersburg until the senate could review his case. He was still waiting, when revolution struck the capital and Alexander I replaced Paul I on the throne.

Czar Paul I had not shown himself to be an enemy of the brotherhood, but if anything, Alexander I was more favorable. In 1804 by decree of Alexander I, the Hasidim were permitted full autonomy in all religious matters and were granted the right to establish their own separate synagogues in which to worship God after their own customs, and they were given the right to appoint rabbis from among their own membership.

Once again the Hasidim were dancing in the streets, shouting for joy and singing songs of praise to God; and this time there was nothing their enemies could do about it.

7

The Occult as a Practical Art

IN THE YEARS following the death of Dov Baer, it became obvious that the possibility of a central Hasidic leadership had shattered and the brotherhood had broken up into distinct dynasties, each embodying divergent points of view. The breakup took place amid anguish and rancor, but from a distance it can be seen as inevitable and good.

Devekut is not the property of a single personality type. What devekut does require is intensity and commitment to the point of abandon. These the Hasid brothers had in abundance. Essentially the brothers shared the same goal, but their individualistic personalities were bound to clash on methodology.

And clash they did in rip-roaring tirades of name-calling and invectives. Some believed that studying holy texts was essential to spiritual growth, some thought it a hindrance, and the rest lined themselves up at various points in between. Some were in favor of meticulous attention to the traditional rituals. Others believed that prayer alone or prayer and devotion to the zaddik was sufficient to achieve personal redemption. There were those who felt it their duty to become involved in community problems. Their opposites felt that true devotion to God could only be achieved in isolation. The Hasid brothers could not even see eye to eye on interpretations of the Bible.

To make the problem of intracommunal peace more difficult, the kind of loyalty that gave the brothers the strength to cling to Hasidism in the face of community persecution made them just as unshakably dedicated to their own beliefs and to the teacher of their choice. More often than not, loyalty to their teacher was the wedge that split one segment of the brotherhood off from the rest. When a beloved teacher died, his disciples were likely to turn to one of the brother disciples for comfort rather than to a man who may have been regarded as a zaddik by their late teacher but was actually a stranger to them. Not only was such a man a stranger, but the nominal zaddik would be teaching from a point of view that was bound to differ in some points with that of their own late teacher. A brother disciple set up as their leader, though he may not have been formally recognized by the brotherhood as a whole, would be teaching a doctrine that was familiar and inspiring.

The splitting of the brotherhood was an act of love, and it may be due to that love that its advantages outweighed the problems that splintering created. For the student of mysticism one of the first advantages it presented was an unexpected highlighting of a large number of unique and diverse mystics.

Holiness is not a common quality. Most generations can count their mystics in ones and twos—if they are lucky enough to have any. And, as we have pointed out, Jewish mystics have shown an extraordinary genius for remaining inconspicuous and unsuspected. Traditionally they reveal themselves only to their peers and their disciples; the rest of their contemporaries can be looking at them and see nothing remarkable. If the Hasidic leadership had been dominated by one man, the amazing Hasid leaders who were pushed into the open by the necessity of taking charge of their splinter groups would have been able to remain invisible to the public eye.

Rarely has the number of holy men in the third generation of Hasidim been found living in the same part of the world at the same time in any other period of history. We are provided with an almost unique opportunity to study the variety of personality types in which holiness can be manifested and the variety of ways in which holiness can manifest itself.

Levi Yitzhok is an example of one of the Maggid's disciples who would have preferred to remain anonymous, leaving the leadership to another. When he died, his disciples refused to go outside their own group for leadership. Since they could not follow one of their master's seed, they took a disciple of Levi Yitzhok's and made him their zaddik.

Elimelech of Lyzhansk, another of Dov Baer's disciples, had a personality as flamboyant as Levi's, but one that worked in quite different ways. He was as generous and as devoted to the causes of poverty and oppression as Levi, but instead of praying and demanding redress of God, Elimelech believed in using his occult powers to wring physical and materialistic good from Nature. His methods are still being ardently supported and furiously disputed today.

He is looked upon as an innovator only by those who wish to pretend the Besht and Dov Baer were not involved in occult activities. In truth Elimelech had not radically altered the teachings and practices of his master or of his master's master. Both the Besht and the Maggid used their occult powers to help those who needed help on the physical plane. It would never have occurred to either of them to turn away someone who came to them to be healed or protected by the use of their occult powers.

Nevertheless, Elimelech is called the creator and theoretician of practical zaddikism as though the Besht and Dov Baer had turned their backs altogether on occultism. He is thought of as the creator because he was espousing the virtues of occultism at a time when it had ceased to be fashionable with many of the young spiritual purists in the brotherhood.

In the days of the Besht and the Maggid it was a rare

intellectual who had been attracted to the brotherhood. Most of the Hasidim were peasants whose hold on life was precarious. Engulfed by poverty, persecution, and ignorance, they accepted any help that came their way with uncritical gratitude. By the third generation Hasidism was also attracting a group of young intellectuals whose needs were less desperate and whose wants were more selective.

Elimelech was an unusual man. An ascetic and extremist by nature, he recognized that the drastic austerities he favored did not suit the temperaments of everybody. Some zaddikim, he believed, achieved redemption through fasting, but some achieved it through eating. The method is good only if it is most effective for the individual. He did believe that a zaddik must be strong enough to keep one foot in the community and the other, so to speak, in heaven. He must concern himself with every aspect of his followers' lives, even the most gross. At the same time it was his duty to use his mystical powers to lift his followers above the gross to the spiritual.

In part a zaddik accomplished these purposes through teaching, prayer, and example, but the larger part was accomplished by means of a specific mystical process. The process is related to Isaac Luria's theory of divine sparks. When a zaddik placed himself on the spiritual level of the lowest member of his community—when he fell, to use his own terminology—energy was generated. This energy helped free the sparks in the souls of those around him so that their souls would rise. The necessary condition for this process is that the zaddik put himself in real metaphysical danger. The agent for redemption must be capable of sin; otherwise, the "descent" or "fall" would not be real.

To be capable of sin, to feel tempted to sin, and then willfully to place oneself on a level with the least spiritual person about is hazardous. But Elimelech did not visualize it in terms of heroics; he felt it was the obligation, the *mitzvah*, of a zaddik to function in this way. The zaddik is rewarded for this function beyond the knowledge of having success-fully done his duty. Each time a zaddik rises from his descent into the murky depths of normal consciousness, he reaches a new height of spiritual attainment. This concept was more food for scandal among the orthodox. The implication that evil could strengthen holiness many rabbis considered an open invitation to sin. But Elimelech saw evil not as a threat but as an opportunity. By elevating or successfully subli-mating sinful thoughts, he believed it was possible to trans-form existence on earth from the profane to the holy. Each of us, he believed, has the power to abolish the dualism of good and evil by transforming evil into good. And if suffi-cient numbers of people accomplish such a transformation, the coming of the Messiah will be at hand.

In his youth Elimelech had wandered about from village to village in ritual imitation of the Shekhinah, helping the needy and accepting just enough for himself for the absolute necessities of life. After Dov Baer's death, he moved to Lyzhansk, Galicia, founded a conventicle, and became its zaddik. He instituted a number of novel customs in his court that were to win wide use and abuse. One of these was the practice of supporting the court and his intimate disciples by means of a kind of tax called the *pidyon*. Pidyon means ransom and refers to the then frequent necessity of giving money to bandits in exchange for kidnapped relatives and friends. The ransom in Elimelech's court and later in the courts of other zaddikim was for a wish that God would grant to those who gave to his holy ones.

Elimelech taught his disciples that a zaddik's function in redemption places him on a higher level than God's seraphim. On earth God fulfills what the zaddik decrees because he is the hope of the world. When he speaks, an angel is formed.

The hope of the world, honored by God, but the role was dangerous and onerous. Eventually, Elimelech withdrew from it, returning to the ascetic life. He locked himself in a room and refused to see anyone except his family and closest disciples and then only on rare occasions. What little food he ate he received through a small window. The rest of the day, every day, there were only walls, a few pieces of furniture, the floor and ceiling, and simple clothing that might distract him from his inner world.

For Elimelech this extreme way of life was not disagreeable but a deliciously dangerous adventure. Like many of his predecessors, he acknowledged the possibility that his heart might fail under the strain of surging joy that he experienced in his prolonged meditations and prayers. However, he felt that redemption was not an absolute gift. During a man's lifetime the redemption he had won slipped away from him like sea water cupped in his hands. He could hold onto it only during the act of prayer. Therefore, in order to experience the joy of living in a state of redemption as much of the time as possible, he risked his life again and again.

Israel ben Shabbetai was another great exponent of practical zaddikism. A list of his teachers reads like a roll call of Hasidic saints: Samuel Horowitz, Elimelech, Levi Yitzhok, and Dov Baer. Like Elimelech, Israel ben Shabbetai had been an ascetic as a boy and as a young man, and a scholar and student of the Kabbalah before he became a Hasid. He idolized the Maggid, saying that he had mastered eight hundred books on the Kabbalah before he had the luck to meet Dov Baer, but at that meeting, suddenly he realized that he knew nothing and must begin to learn about mysticism from the starting point.

A preacher, he was renowned for the elegance and lucidity of his sermons. He was a man who could hold a widely divergent audience spellbound. He had something for them all: proverbs for the peasants, Kabbalistic symbolism for the mystics and poets, and impeccable logic for the scholars. After Dov Baer's death, he devoted himself to the brotherhood and to improving the lives of the poor, especially those of their children. He made prodigious use of his occult powers in healing and protecting from harm those who came to him for help.

Practical zaddikism implies concern for the problems of everyday life, but Israel ben Shabbetai's attention to these matters never drew his interest away from his spiritual mission. He believed a zaddik's principal duty was to bring men closer to God. Although he knew teaching and counseling were helpful, he was convinced that the key to spiritual development of his followers was his own devotion to God.

Israel ben Shabbetai was a spiritual elitist. Not all men—in fact few men—could attain the heights of those who were born to become zaddikim. Since the zaddik had special talents, he felt, he had the obligation to use his devotion to God as a kind of slipstream to suck along those around him to redemption.

Just as devoted to Dov Baer as were his other disciples, Aryeh Leib Sarahs was different from them all. Even his name is unique. As we have seen, in those days a man was named by his given name and that of his father: Israel ben Shabbetai, Israel, the son of Shabbetai. But Aryeh carried his mother's name: Aryeh, the son of Sarah. He was the disciple who went to the Maggid not to hear him preach the Torah but to watch him tie his bootlaces. The phrase almost sums up his life. He refused to preside over a court or to elevate himself in any way. He did not preach. He did not theorize. He spent his life wandering across the countryside, giving comfort to those he met, collecting money to secure the release of prisoners, especially those pathetic men who had been imprisoned for no other crime than being too poor to pay their debts. He had become a Hasid because of his love for Dov Baer, but he remained an old-style mystic, preferring not to reveal himself to those around him.

Samuel Shnelke Horowitz was a very different kind of personality. By nature he was a politician and diplomat. He made of himself a badly needed bridge between the boisterous brotherhood and the community at large, preparing the ground for wider acceptance of Hasidic principles by introducing them gradually to those he contacted; he also scouted within the orthodox community for young men who were ripe for a commitment to Hasidism and directed them to Dov Baer and other Hasidic teachers.

His low profile was not only a tactic but an expression of his character. Often he expressed disapproval of the hilarity and rowdyism at the Hasidic courts.

His younger brother, Phenehas Horowitz, was even more ambivalent about the Hasidic method. Phenehas had studied first under his father and then under his older brothers before Samuel took him along to listen to Dov Baer. For a while he came strongly under the Maggid's spell, but his conservatism asserted itself after he filled the position of rabbi in Frankfurt, Germany. There, his negative feelings about Hasidism grew more deep year after year. Finally, they led him to join in banning Rabbi Rathon Alder from religious functions due to his Hasidic leanings. Mysticism pulled on Phenehas like a lost love. He fought the desire, however, and warned his students not to give in to the ideas of the Hasidim.

Samuel was every bit as ascetic as his younger brother and certainly as socially respectable in his post of head rabbi for the province of Nikolsburg, Moravia, a position confirmed by the Empress Maria Theresa herself. Despite his anxieties about the dangers that the radical methodology might lead him into, he continued his studies and practiced both occult and mystical disciplines. His efforts on behalf of the brotherhood did much to spread Hasidism throughout Poland and into Galicia.

Meshulam Zusya of Hanipoli, another of the Maggid's disciples, was the brother of Elimelech of Lyzhansk and one of the great heroes of Hasidic folk literature. The stories about him always describe him as unlearned, almost ignorant, and not too bright, but filled with such purity of intention and goodness that he finds favor in God's sight. Samples of Meshulam's writings still exist, and they show him to have been a scholar who knew his Torah well. He renounced intellectual achievements for a life of service to the poor. In the beginning, Meshulam moved from place to place in the footsteps of the early Kabbalistic mystics. In spite of his modest ways he was very influential with the brothers and, interestingly enough, in the face of his antiintellectualism, he became a close friend of the scholarly Shneur Zalman.

After Dov Baer's death, Meshulam settled in Hanipoli, directing the spiritual life of a small group of followers. He and his brother were close all their lives, often traveling together in their youth, and when Elimelech died, quite a few of his disciples moved to Hanipoli to study under Meshulam. After his death, the group in Hanipoli asked his oldest son Menahem Zevi Hirsh to be their leader. Meshulam's youngest son Israel Abraham served as the Hasidic rabbi in Chernyostrov. When he died his wife assumed the leadership of the Cherny Ostrov group for several years.

Aaron ben Jacob of Karlin, although a disciple of the Maggid's, was another who initiated radical changes in the Hasidic method. He vehemently opposed the antiascetic rebellion that the Besht had begun. When Aaron became a zaddik, he demanded rigid ascetic discipline of his disciples. Each of them was required to spend one day of the week in complete seclusion, fasting in a special room set aside for that purpose. During the time of seclusion, the disciple was to devote his time to repentance and study of the Torah and other holy works. A strong believer in scholarship, Aaron expected his students to read the *mishnah* daily and to master the Bible. Even more surprising from a Hasid, however, was his bleak focusing on sin and the need to repent. Dour by nature, he frequently warned his followers of the dangers of pride and anger, as well as those of ignorance and venality. He spoke against melancholy, too, but from a typical point of view, noting that joy stems from sanctity.

Music was perhaps Aaron's only soft spot on the sensuous plane. He was enthusiastic about its ability to develop concentration (*kavanah*), which is the prime prerequisite of devekut. His hymn for the Sabbath is still being sung. The first line of the hymn, "O God, I yearn for the Sabbath's delight," provides a hint of the zest of the man and suggests why, despite his strictness, his followers worshipped him. They called him Aaron the Great and it was his personality with all its dour repressiveness that was responsible for the spread of Hasidism into that long-time holdout for the brotherhood, Lithuania. The Lithuanians acknowledged the relationship by calling their Hasidim Karliners.

Aaron was not an occultist, but he was committed to community problems, using political and social methods to accomplish his purposes. He started his political activities under Dov Baer when, as the Maggid's emissary, he was able to effect tax relief for the poor. Thanks to his encouragement, groups of Karliners settled in the Holy Land both in Tiberias and in Jerusalem. When Aaron the Great died, his followers refused to recognize another of Dov Baer's disciples as their zaddik. They asked their late leader's disciple Solomon ben Mein to take over the role.

The succession of this dynasty is particularly helpful in understanding the flexibility of the brotherhoods. Each zaddik, though limited to some extent by custom and ceremonialized procedure, nevertheless has great scope in developing his own programs and theories. The brotherhoods tend to place their confidence more in the holiness of their zaddikim than in set formula.

Along with Aaron the Great's followers, his son Asher became a disciple of Solomon and eventually took command of his father's dynasty.

Although from the outside, the disciplined, scholarly Shneur Zalman would seem to have had much in common with Aaron's approach to spiritual life, Asher opposed his concept of Hasidism, supporting instead Abraham of Kalish. Like Shneur Zalman, he felt the effects of falling under the suspicions of the Christian government. In 1798 he and his disciples were imprisoned, but eventually they were released.

Asher became famous for the emphasis he placed on productive work. Efficient work habits develop character and spirituality. Laziness can become habitual, he warned. The man who allows himself to be negligent in his secular duties will end being negligent in his religious life as well. With unusual insight into the effect of persecution upon an individual's ethical standards, Asher warned his disciples to refrain from avenging themselves on their persecutors by exploiting Christians who were working for them.

While Asher watched over the brotherhood in Stolen, Solomon ben Mein traveled to Lodomeria, taking with him Asher's son, who like his father before him was studying under Solomon. The two men established a conventicle in Lodomeria.

When Asher died, his son succeeded him and Lodomeria became the headquarters for the Karliners. Aaron II, like his grandfather, emphasized the combination of prayer and study. He told his disciples that God does not count the pages they finished but the hours they spent reading the Torah. However, he did not emphasize physical asceticism, unlike Aaron. He believed that repentance grows out of joy and delight in God. He urged his followers to make a worship out of their daily life. Worship and sincerity in prayer were enough to attain the perfection needed to bring about the messianic era. He watched over the brotherhood with a fatherly eye, developing the custom of writing letters to his followers just before the Festival of Passover. Those letters were a badly needed source of encouragement in the grim days of Czar Nicholas II.

Aaron II was succeeded by his son Asher II, who was one of the first Hasidic zaddikim to emphasize purely physical ritual. He felt that the physical ritual of purification of the body would in itself have the effect of developing sanctity. He ordered his disciples—winter or summer—to observe the ancient custom of immersing themselves in sanctified water. When Asher II's career was cut short by his early death, his followers refused to accept as zaddik anyone not of his seed. Accordingly, to the scandal of the community, they formally set his four-year-old son Israel upon his empty throne.

Known as the Babe of Stolin, after Israel reached the

age when he could assume real authority, surprisingly, he more than fulfilled his followers' anticipation of excellence. He put great effort into encouraging his followers to work smoothly and harmoniously with non-Hasidim whether Jew or Christian. And in an age when women were expected to be chaste and humble, and not much more, Israel stressed the importance of educating young girls belonging to the brotherhood, saying that its women were the foundation of Judaism. He was effective as a father as well as a leader. In Stolin he was succeeded by his first-born son Moses, and three other of his sons carried on the tradition of Karlin Hasidism. Abraham Elimelech, his second son, became the rabbi at Karlin. His third son Johanan served as the Hasidic rabbi in Lutsk, Volhynia. And Jacob, his fourth son, brought Karlin Hasidism to the United States.

Both Moses and Abraham founded Hasidic schools and worked hard to keep the far-flung Karliners united. Their efforts were destroyed along with their lives and those of thousands of other Hasidim in Hitler's bloodbath. After World War II, Johanan too came to the United States. When he died, there was no son to take his place. His followers, wishing to continue his line, began educating his young grandson for that role; however, at that time some of the Karlin Hasidim preferred to join the Lelov dynasty.

In rare instances, strong rivalry broke out between master and disciple. Jacob Isaac, another of Dov Baer's disciples, had a temperament that provoked this type of dispute and brought about two additional dynasties in the Hasidic brotherhood.

After the Maggid's death Jacob Isaac became the disciple of Elimelech of Lyzhansk. Although his later teachings and his life-style appear to owe much to Elimelech, master and student quarreled bitterly, so bitterly that while his master still was alive and active, Jacob Isaac founded a court of his own in Lublin and eventually attracted hundreds of followers in Poland and Galicia. His extraordinary occult powers earned him the title, Seer of Lublin. Like the Besht, he could read character in a man's face and predict events yet to come. It was also said of him that he could discover the genealogy of a person's soul and learn when, during each stage of reincarnation, his soul had achieved redemption.

Called "Everyone's Rabbi," he attracted men from all social levels. No scholar himself, he brushed aside intellectual endeavor. Joyful prayer, he felt, was the single most important answer to success. Like Elimelech, Jacob Isaac stressed the duty of the zaddik to help his followers on a material level. He felt that poverty weighs down a person's soul and that by devoting time and energy to improve the living conditions of his followers, he was at the same time assisting their spiritual lives. He liked to say, when the body enjoys, the soul can enjoy spiritual richness.

Man's relationship to his fellow man is also an important part of his spiritual development, Jacob Isaac thought. Love of others and humility about oneself were constant themes of his. One of his famous disciples, David ben Solomon of Lelov, who eventually established a dynasty of his own, was echoing his master's teachings when he lamented to his followers that he was not worthy to be a zaddik because he still cared more for his own child than for the children of others.

Jacob Isaac was a tireless teacher and extraordinarily popular. Although no son of his continued his line, in the first half of the nineteenth century, most of the Hasidic zaddikim in Poland and Galicia had studied under him. Eventually, however, the Seer was to suffer as he had made his master suffer. His disciple Jacob Isaac ben Asher quarreled with him and founded a court of his own, instituting a new variation of the Hasidic method called Pshishhah Hasidism, the New Path in Hasidism. For the disciple's part the quarrel was largely a matter of principle. He tried valiantly to restore friendly relations with his master but the Seer was bitter about the defection and refused to be reconciled with him.

Jacob Isaac ben Asher, the disciple, had come from a famous rabbinical family and had been given a scholar's education before discovering his master and becoming a Hasid. More than a scholar already, he had given away much of his family's inheritance, and was supporting himself by teaching school while continuing his studies and his mystical exercises. For a time he was the Seer's most devoted disciple. The Seer returned the affection, respecting his scholastic abilities. Eventually, he entrusted the young man with the responsibility of acting as spiritual counselor for the scholars who had come to study under him. No doubt it was this very responsibility that ultimately precipitated the break. As he directed his own attention to factors that helped the young students in his charge and to factors that distracted or slowed down their progress, he began forming his own theories about mystical discipline and discovered, no doubt to his dismay, that they did not coincide with the theories of the Seer.

Jacob Isaac ben Asher was an austere taskmaster. He told the boys that there was no standing still in life; one either worked hard or deteriorated. And he was alert for the slightest signs of deterioration. At the same time he watched just as vigilantly for spiritual vanity. Despite his strictness or because of it, his charges adored him, giving him the nickname, the Holy Jew.

Where the Holy Jew and the Seer came to verbal blows was on the issue of occultism. Jacob Isaac ben Asher felt that desire to possess such powers represented a powerful temptation luring the young men away from concentration on mystical studies. The Seer believed that his powers were a gift from God to be used for the benefit of the community. The Holy Jew felt that his zaddik's use of occult powers was perverting his court. Master and disciple could not agree, and neither was the kind of man to compromise.

Finally Jacob Isaac ben Asher left the Seer's court, taking with him some of the young men he had been instructing. The new group settled down in Przysucha, with the Holy Jew assuming the role of zaddik and inaugurating the program that earned the title the New Path in Hasidism.

The New Path stressed scholarship and discipline, and completely disavowed occultism. The Holy Jew was fond of telling his disciples that at a certain level of spiritual development, anyone could perform wonders. What is difficult, he believed, because it requires patient, consistent vigilance, is fulfilling one's obligations as a human being; but difficult as it is, if one succeeds, redemption is certain.

Jacob Isaac ben Asher was an ascetic. Before becoming a Hasid, he had seriously weakened, with prolonged fasts and sleepless, prayerful nights, what had been a healthy, strong body. Although he tempered his regime while studying under the Seer, he never entirely gave it up.

He was also a perfectionist. It is not surprising in view of his personality that he taught methods of developing the ability to concentrate and stressed the value of ethical behavior rather than emphasized devotion. The level of concentration he considered adequate, not excellent, he defined as that of a man who when saying his prayer would not feel pain if he were stabbed by a sword. Needless to say, few of his initiates measured up to his standards. Nevertheless this level was his goal. He never wavered and never stopped holding it up in front of his disciples: total absorption during meditation to the point of complete loss of contact with bodily sensation. Anything less was a failure. Obviously, that type of concentration is not easily achieved, and for this reason, the Holy Jew and his followers never placed importance on punctuality. Quality of performance, not ritual correctness, was the aim.

By this time some of the brotherhoods had changed sufficiently; they had become more conservative and gone back to a greater reliance on ritual, so that even they were scandalized by the Pshishhah Hasidim's disregard of the conventions. Tempers flared and friendships were forgotten in the torrent of debate and recrimination. The disciples of the Seer, still angry at Jacob Isaac ben Asher for leaving them, were especially vituperative. And the Seer, whose temper almost matched his devotion to God, joined heartily in the fray.

Today we can see the dispute as a demonstration that spiritual life is open to men of widely differing personality types. For all his holiness, Jacob Isaac ben Asher regarded love of one's fellows as a duty. He seems to have been one of those disciplined, earnest individuals not basically affectionate by nature. His master—warm, passionate, impatient of restraints—was almost his opposite. Their temperaments diverged; their ultimate goals were the same. Each achieved that goal but each had to find his own means, the method most suited to his own capacity.

The Hasidic brothers of this third generation were extraordinary men. They had personalities as strong as garlic and vinegar, champagne and maple syrup—and just as varied. They used their personalities to explore differing patterns of mysticism, and when holiness came, it was reflected through their individual natures; holiness did not reduce them to the neutral blandness of a Sunday school character.

8

Growing up in a Hasidic Family

FIFTY YEARS AFTER the death of the Baal Shem Tov, Hasidism had become the dominant religious expression for most of Jewish eastern Europe. In Germany, Russia, and Palestine, Hasidim danced in the courts of their zaddikim. By this time the pattern of Hasidic life had shaped itself and hardened. The brotherhood that had begun as an evangelical movement had become largely hereditary. A Hasid was born not only into the larger brotherhood but into the following of the zaddik of his father. Loyalties were fierce, and defections almost unknown. The rights of the Hasidim to follow their own practices were acknowledged. Discrimination was rare. Even the prejudice had died down. The Hasidim were not, however, integrated into the community. They maintained their own places of worship. They organized their own heders or arranged for Hasidic tutoring of their children. Even their friendships and social life were conducted almost entirely within the framework of the Hasidic dynasty of their birth. Marriages were still arranged; and with the hope of children, the arrangement was almost never outside the dynastic communality.

Within the dynastic brotherhoods, life was familiar and intimate. Families lived comfortably in each other's homes. Even where population of the dynasty was thin, there was traveling back and forth and long visits with relatives and friends. The children grew up in each other's eyesight, playing, studying, and working together, so that in each generation the term brotherhood had real sociological meaning.

Their early persecution had created a custom of sharing that had become one of the great beauties of the movement. The feeling of being brothers, of belonging to a large family, was strong. Hasidim attending the same zaddik could be certain of a welcome in the home of a brother Hasid even if they were from different parts of the world and strangers. The rich helped the poor with gifts of money and the use of their possessions. More important than material gifts was the lack of stigma in being poor. A humble man entered the homes of his rich brothers through the main door and was invited to sit beside them in their carriages without being made to feel that his dirty clothes and muddy boots defiled the furnishings. The Hasidim's pride was in their zaddik, and their competitiveness was channeled along religious lines. In that area a poor man could be as good as his wealthy neighbor.

Wherever they lived, no matter how far away, the eyes of a Hasid were on the court of his zaddik. That was the heart of spiritual life, both mystically and physically. Nearby, if numbers and circumstances permitted it, the brothers built a place of worship that they called a stibble. Unlike most of the imposing European synagogues, the stibble reflected the Hasidic communal feeling. Half temple, yes, but also half hostel, the stibble contained a sleeping room for travelers, a dining room, and a social hall. Often the building was as dingy and poorly lighted as a peasant's hut, but it generated warmth and inclusiveness. It belonged to all the brotherhood. No one was shy of entering its doors. The farmer and the poor craftsman were not ashamed to hurry to worship without first robbing themselves of precious time and energy by changing into their Sabbath clothes. The stibble was always open. The old men, too frail for the fields, would go there to sit and smoke and reminisce. In surroundings so much like their own homes, it was easier to avoid self-consciousness and to lose themselves completely in prayer. After services, they gathered in the hall, drank some wine or brandy, and sang Hasidic songs until joy started them dancing. The stibble was ugly only on the outside.

Hasid education tended to produce a happier child than the standard European heder, although, of course, this tendency varied somewhat from dynasty to dynasty. With their emphasis on emotion and their use of motion in worship, Hasid children were not forced to become elders before they had known the exuberance of youth.

Instead of being set to memorize long passages from the Torah and forced to remain silent when not reciting, the children were taught their heritage through songs and stories. Dancing and playing were not as likely to be frowned upon. A laughing face was considered beautiful in the sight of God and a happy heart an important condition for worship. More important, unlike many of the Jews and Christians of their time, Hasidic children were not thought to have been born sinners. Hasidim felt that their lives played an important role in God's plan for redemption and that each of their children was born for this special task. They grew up with the dignity of one who has an important purpose to accomplish. Good character was expected of them. And they were guided toward devekut from early childhood. A child with a natural bent toward scholarship would be given books to study—the Torah, the Zohar, and other holy books of Judaism. But a child whose life was in the workings of his hands, the strength of his back, or the keen-eyed shrewdness needed in the marketplace was praised for his skills, and was taught how to combine with his talent a love of God.

In those days among the nineteenth-century Hasidim, the *Bar Mitzvah* literally signaled the ending of childhood and the entering into man's estate, and the gap from Bar Mitzvah to marriage ceremony was not usually a large one. The brotherhood had a reputation for marrying its children young in an age that considered an unmarried girl of twenty a spinster.

The Bar Mitzvah ceremony was celebrated in the stibble with great rejoicing among family and friends around the countryside. As soon after the ceremony as possible, the son was taken by his father for a formal introduction to his zaddik. Usually, his first visit to the man who was to be the dominant figure in his world was likely to be the most awesome experience of his life. More likely than not, in order to reach the court, they had a long, eventful trip, probably by carriage. The dynasties were spread out through villages, towns, and often across national boundaries.

Even if the boy came from an affluent family, the splendor of the zaddik's court was certain to impress him. And when he met the zaddik dressed in his robes, treated with great deference by his father and all the other men about him, excitement choked the words in his throat.

At the initial meeting the zaddik spoke and touched the boy, blessing him. There was more to come. The visit was prolonged over weeks and months. The boy lived at court, sleeping with other young men who were visitors like himself or who belonged to the court. Often they slept on wooden benches and supped only on soup with a bit of meat in it for their main meal. But the time itself was delicious beyond delicacies. It must have been a little like going to heaven while still alive. The air was filled with mysticism. Conversation hovered around techniques of prayer, methods of concentration, stories of visions and powers and saints. And his instruction was taking place at the pinnacle of his world. He could go there again, but he would never go to a more important place or visit a more important personage in his life.

It was not all hard work and solemnity. A steady stream of visitors poured through the court from all parts of Europe and even from Palestine itself. Wealthy merchants brushed up against beggars, scholars, artisans, invalids, government officials, sightseers, and pious brother Hasidim of every age.

There were strange costumes and customs to see and stranger tales to listen to.

The very city that held the court buzzed with the constant ebb and flow of departures, newcomers seeking lodging, friends meeting unexpectedly on the streets, business deals consummated, Hasidic tales, political discussions, and scholarly debates tossed back and forth. The holiday air was so strong that even strangers greeted each other familiarly with cries of *Shalom Aleichem*. The city that could boast a Hasidic court could plan on a lush flow of tourist revenue. In Catholic Poland cities came openly to compete with each other for the patronage that meant prosperity, and a city favored with the occupancy of a zaddik's court saw to it that its ordinances and law enforcers made the Hasidim feel comfortable within their urban jurisdiction. In addition to his other impressions, the boy's estimation of the standing of his brotherhood in the world was certain to rise during this visit.

For all the reverence and the hours spent in prayer and talk about praying with spiritual counselors, there were the usual Hasidic songs and dances and acrobatics for the joy of God. Alcohol, too, was certain to be consumed, at least after the awesome third meal of Sabbath. In some courts it would be as little as a ritual sip. But in many, enough toasts would be downed so that after the exertion and emotion, the visitor would go to sleep that night with his head spinning.

Even the son of the poorest member of the community was able to enjoy this period of visitation. The brotherhood provided money—*tikun*, as it was called—for the support of those who lived at court. And it was not unusual that a boy whose hands had never held a coin knew a luxuriant jingle in his purse while at court.

Normally this time of times lasted a quarter of a year at the most. Not a long period in relation to a lifespan, but sufficient for the purpose. Sufficient to confirm the inner man in his dedication to a life of the spirit. Sufficient to set his loyalty firmly with the dynasty. Sufficient to convince managed the court formalities were chosen from the ranks of the yoshbim. These positions were power roles within the ranks of the brotherhood, for it was the officials who decided who should be privileged to see the zaddik privately and how much time would be allotted to him.

The yoshbim formed the zaddik's spiritual family, an important source of human intimacy and personal affection for the leader. In addition to the mystical benefits derived from the relationship, it was possible to acquire materialistic advantages as well for those whose personalities permitted them to harvest such opportunities. Zaddikim were known for their paternal regard of their fledglings. After family pressure had forced them to leave court, favorable positions, likely business, and marketing arrangements that came to the zaddik's attention were shunted their way, directly as the result of the zaddik's personal intervention or indirectly by men who knew their leader would look kindly upon those who helped his favorites.

No doubt many sharp-eyed entrepreneurs have hidden under the robes of a yoshbi, going through the motions of spirituality, deliberately pretending a devotion they did not feel. For all that, the majority of the yoshbim were what they seemed to be on the surface: young mystics who adored their teachers and wanted nothing more than to serve them and to hear from them how best to serve God.

Regardless of how spectacularly the yoshbi's spiritual development progressed, in the normal course of events, he was not destined to become a zaddik. That exalted position was reserved for the zaddik's first-born son. Back of all the Hasidic dynasties lies the belief that holiness is as inheritable as blue eyes. As we have seen, it is a dogma that was accepted in the third generation of zaddikim. Neither Israel Baal Shem Tov nor Dov Baer gave any evidence of having believed in divine heredity.

Whether the belief of the third-generation zaddikim—and not all of them subscribed to the belief—is warranted is a matter for personal conviction. It seems to us that the great-the boy that he was a man. He returned home altered, not enormously, for human personality is slow in growing, but enough to impress him with himself. And the new pattern was confirmed when he entered the village and found himself welcomed on equal terms to the fellowship of men, in fact, treated as a celebrity, rich as he was in gossip about the zaddik, the court life, and their distant friends.

Occasionally the visitation to court stimulated a fierce spiritual awakening. In such cases the zaddik kept the boy with him indefinitely—as long as his family could spare the young man and sometimes longer. There are many tales of young women effectively widowed by their husbands' devotion to the zaddik. In theory, the young wives were honored and pleased by their husbands' grace in the sight of God. No doubt there were those whose personal spirituality and unselfishness were equal to the expectation. And the communal life of the Hasid helped to keep those court-widows from the raw feeling of aloneness they would experience in our society. Nevertheless, for the court-widow who was young and without her man, prevented by her status from finding another, although nominally a matron economically under her parent's authority and probably under their roof, disappointment must often have festered into bitterness and chronic resentment. When through their fathers' intercession, the young wives were able to repossess their mates, they achieved at best a chancy household with a husband whose mind and heart were elsewhere. Often for as long as the zaddik lived, the husband-disciple kept slipping back for prolonged visits, leaving his family to struggle along as best they could; and even when he returned, such an otherworldly man rarely showed talent in supplying material necessities. Within the boundaries of Hasidic marriage customs, it takes a saint to be married happily to a holy man.

The young follower who comes to live at court to become the zaddik's disciple is called a *yoshbi*. His life becomes dominated by prayer; personal service to the zaddik; and a lesser amount of study of the Torah, the Lurian commentaries, and Hasidic literature. The officials who est disadvantage is not that it places on the throne of authority those who are not holy but that it automatically eliminates many who are holy and perhaps more qualified for the position in other ways. However, hereditary succession has to a large extent prevented the office from becoming subject to the kind of politics that surrounds the selecting of a pope, for example. That in itself may be sufficient advantage for the arrangement. From the standpoint of many exalted mystics a further advantage may well be that having the brotherhood's attention on their leader shields them from the spotlight of reverence and allows them to live their days quietly in prayerful exultation.

The comparison of the zaddik with the pope is a fair one on an organizational level at least, for in many ways they have similar powers. The zaddik has the right to change the torah by which the Hasidim live, for he is the living personification of God's Torah. Through his person the life force that animates the universe flows, that is to say, the Shekhinah or sparks from the Shekhinah. The same life force flows through us all, but most if not all of the dynasties subscribe to the elitist theory that the zaddik is empowered by substantially larger amounts of the deity than are his followers. Due to that greater proportion of divinity to flesh, he has power over both the visible and the invisible worlds and has access to the sum total of earthly and occult knowledge.

The degree to which the dynastic leaders practice occult arts varies with the dynasty. Those zaddikim who refrain from occultism do so as a form of asceticism; they are denying themselves the use of power that they know is theirs to use.

The heredity that forms the basis for zaddikism is not based on the genetic theory that governs fleshly form, even though the end result is much the same. Rather, it is brought about at the moment of conception by the holiness of the zaddik and the purity and spiritualization of the sexual union. His sanctity is passed on to his sons in their mother's womb. God showers his grace upon the unborn saintling, bestowing upon him illumination of the soul. His future redemption is predestined. Even as an infant, he may not be judged by common human standards. His flesh has been purified by its contact with the spiritual force within.

Those claims sound blatant, even false, to Westerners who are more given to glorifying movie stars and athletes than their religious leaders. The objective truth in the claims of zaddikism is probably impossible to obtain. Fortunately, the problem works out rather well. Those people who demand objective proof most vigorously are really not interested in spiritual development. Their interest and faith lie in the material world that can provide them with all the objective proof they desire. And contrariwise, those who do seek spiritual adventure are willing to explore new possibilities on the gamble that the legends and tales and rumors have something besides noise behind them.

It has been demonstrated again and again that one of the easiest, quickest, and most pleasant ways of acquiring personal piety is by loving devotedly a living man who is holy. Love of the ordinary sort between close friends or parent and child seems to form a kind of psychic channel through which piety can flow. For this reason holy men of all faiths and in every age have emphasized the importance to their disciples that the disciples love and serve them.

This invitation is the opposite of self-serving. Devotion is a grave responsibility on the part of the loved one. It may be an accrual of spiritual hardship, for some say that the sins of the disciples are burdens their master "contracts" to lift up before he himself may be wholly redeemed. It will be remembered that the Baal Shem Tov, one of the least self-seeking men the world has seen, stressed the importance of the zaddik's role.

The issue of self-serving and vanity rests on the fulcrum of holiness. A relationship that is nourishing to the disciple and praiseworthy in the master if he is holy becomes decadent and dangerous if he is not—dangerous to disciple and master both. The disciple becomes a pawn in his master's self-glorification; the master falls from temptation to temptation, with each yielding becoming more vain, contemptuous, and coldly calculating. None of these characteristics make fertile soil for devotion to God. Eventually that devotion too withers and then the master and those who serve him are truly lost.

Corruption

9

THE NINETEENTH CENTURY was not a vintage time for the Hasidim. The shift from the evangelism of the first two generations to the dynastic zaddikism of the third placed enormous responsibility on a very few men. That responsibility coupled with the wildfire growth in numbers of the brothers meant that the ordinary human frailties of those men were multiplied by the thousands of their followers, and shadowed the vast territories in which their influence was felt.

The display that had begun with Dov Baer's white satin robes had become more pronounced generation after generation until glamor and pretense dominated too many of the Hasidic courts. Precedence to the wealthy and the powerful whose donations supported the opulence and splendor of the zaddikim made its appearance and finally became accepted practice. Once again the peasants and poor villagers were hustled through their audiences and shoved to the rear of the worship hall.

In some dynasties interest in making money was as keen as in any merchant family. Even the zaddik's annual blessing to his followers was often bent into a means of extracting money.

With the growth of membership in the brotherhoods, the ability of the zaddik to supervise personally the spiritual life of each of his followers had diminished considerably.

There were too many followers to remember them all by face and name, far less their more important inner characteristics. Even if it were not for the numbers that stood between the average Hasid and his zaddik, distance and travel conditions would have made frequent association impossible.

In many of the dynasties, a hundred years after the Besht's death, the Hasid was as isolated from his zaddik as the peasant had been from his rabbi when the Besht began his religious reform. Once a year the Hasidim met with their leader on the occasion of the high holy days—Rosh Hashanah to Yom Kippur. Even this visit involved sufficient sacrifice that it had to be made obligatory, a religious duty that had to be fulfilled on pain of grave consequences to the soul if one failed. Too remote and too much of a figurehead to hold prolonged conversation with most of his followers, the zaddik had formalized the meeting and simplified it to the point of an exchange of blessing from him for a donation accompanied by a prayer note on which a wish was written. The rich gave more than the poor, but everyone gave.

More likely than not, the prayer note requested materialistic gratifications. A typical one might read: With the Grace of God, Yussel, the son of Rebekah, that he may prosper in business. Another familiar request read: With the Grace of God, Benjamin for his daughter Leah that she might be delivered of a son. To these prayer notes the zaddik answered, after he had read them, "The Holy One, blessed be He, will help you." The reply rarely varied. If a desperate man pleaded for details of the forthcoming help, he was likely to receive a frown and a repetition of the formula.

It was cold, ritualistic comfort and whether it was accompanied by a thrust of mystical force lifting the follower's soul upward doubtless varied from zaddik to zaddik. Some of the accounts make one suspect that certain zaddikim during this period had less spiritual force than their average follower.

To some the distances and time involved represented a terrible austerity, requiring the pawning of precious family goods. However, nothing, not even the extremes of poverty, justified remaining away from court.

If the follower did not receive adequate compensation in terms of spirituality or help with his material problems, he did obtain more than his share of awe. Imagine a peasant watching open-mouthed as his zaddik is driven through the city streets in a gold-gilt-covered carriage drawn by a team of snorting thoroughbreds that are handled by uniformed drivers accompanied by a pair of elegant footmen. In architectural magnificence the zaddik's palace frequently rivaled those of the country's noblemen. The zaddik's dress was a masterpiece of tailoring and fine material. Most of the zaddikim looked and lived like princes. They had been born in a palace, spent their days in a palace, and were to die there.

They may or may not have been mystics. But how could these men have known the hearts of their followers, so many of whom worked in the fields or in grubby huts plying a trade. Men and women who had been a little undernourished all their lives, who had been tired all their lives, who had been frightened and resentful all their lives, who had been oppressed by the same Christians who welcomed the wealthy zaddik with smiling faces—how could the zaddik know the words to comfort them? How could he know the temptations that bore hard on them? Unless he were truly telepathic and truly mystical, no matter how good his intentions, he could not know.

The average follower was not even allowed to worship with his zaddik during these annual visits. The Maggid's rule of isolation rather than the Besht's of intimacy had become the pattern. For the zaddik there was a room kept for his worship alone. The room was inside the synagogue where the Hasidim prayed, but it was hidden from their view. The only contact his followers had with him during prayer were the signals he gave his reader indicating when to proceed and when to pause in the service.

During the visitation, even visual contact was kept at a minimum. During the week that stretched between Rosh Hashanah and Yom Kippur, the zaddik remained aloof from the community. At the advent of Sabbath, his expectant followers lined up, pushing and crowding for a position of vantage. When their leader appeared, fresh from his ablutions, a disciple preceded him, bent over as though serving a king, cleaning with a cloth the path before his master's feet. As the zaddik advanced, his worshiping followers fell back, opening a passage through which he passed in slow, solemn dignity. Often during this appearance the zaddik kept his face covered with his prayer shawl, allowing only his eyes to be seen.

It was marvelous theater, but what would the Besht have thought?

The greatest intimacy with their zaddik that his followers knew came during the Sabbath meals and these too seem to have been more theater than a genuine reaching out to contact his people.

The first meal on Friday night was called the Meal of Our Father Abraham. The meal was more ritual than nourishment; the community was expected to assuage its hunger beforehand. Long banquet tables were set for these occasions. The followers gathered at the synagogue, making their way to the tables, finding their places with tense whispers and escalating excitement. At the head of the zaddik's table, the Sabbath bread sat awaiting benediction. The zaddik entered, and the room became silent. He washed his hands in ceremonial formality and pronounced his blessing. Then with the same ceremony, he picked up a loaf of bread and, tearing off bits of it, passed these to his favorites. The room was taut with expectant silence. The zaddik neither spoke nor looked around the sea of faces that stared intently at him. The women brought in large bowls of soup. After the soup came platters of fish, a food that has mystical meaning in Kabbalistic symbolism. Naturally, the zaddik was served first. He selected a mouthful and silently motioned the women away.

Mayhem was loosed. The zaddik's touch sanctified the fish. Now it was called *shirayim*—the remains—and possessed the combined significance of relic and communion wafer. Young and old, rich and poor, the Hasidim scrambled, pulled, pushed, grunted in their reckless efforts to obtain for themselves this blessing in a physical form.

After the exuberance of the fish course, the meat was eaten in formality that permitted the old men to catch their breath. Brandy finished off the meal and the singing began. Again the community tension burst out in passionate release. The Hasidim moved as they sang, torsos swaying, arms flying, heads tossing. Some, overcome with emotion, left their chairs for ecstatic leaps and dizzying somersaults. Their zaddik, watching this orgy of joy, participated, if at all, by a slight inclination of his head to the song's rhythm or by humming softly a few of its bars.

Quiet was restored when the zaddik's attendants came in carrying a glass of wine which the zaddik blessed, sipped, and handed back to be passed on to the faithful as another form of "remains."

After Saturday morning services, the Meal of Our Father Isaac was held. The followers gathered together, but they were not blessed by their leader's presence. In his place he sent more shirayim, perhaps a *kugel,* minus one bite, to be fought over and treasured.

When the sun was setting on the Sabbath, after the first evening service, the Hasidim celebrated the Departure of Queen Sabbath with the Meal of Our Father Jacob. It was a solemn occasion and the meal was marked by great reverence and believed to impart spiritual benefits. The meal, consisting of a solitary dish of fish, was served in darkness and awed silence. Each Hasid forced himself to swallow at least one mouthful of the symbolic flesh. As darkness began to settle in, the zaddik's voice rose, chanting a hymn. His followers took up the chant, moving their bodies rhythmically as they sang. Even after the voices fell silent, the Hasidim sat, heads turned to where their leader, almost invisible in the gathering darkness, seemed to be meditating. Finally, the attendants lit candles and the zaddik stood before his Hasidim to give his torah. These were essentially the only words his followers had had from him during the expensive week and they listened with close attention. Every word, every expression was memorized, and often later written down, to be repeated and speculated over in their village stibbles throughout the year to come. The ritual ended with singing of psalms. Often the zaddik himself sang Psalm 121. After the singing, he chanted the *Habdalah* over a glass of wine, uttered a prayer—the Yiddish prayer of Levi Yitzhok was a favorite—and once more secluded himself.

At midnight of that day the Hasidim gathered again for the Feast of King David. This ceremony often gave the brotherhoods a bad name with the more conventional members of their communities. Each family brought its own refreshments, usually brandy and some herring, and the zaddik watched while his people sang and danced and shouted and sometimes got a little drunk. Often the celebrating continued until the hour farm folk began waking up.

Drunkenness is not a characteristic of the Hasidim, but the brotherhood was born in a part of the world and at a time when hard drinking was part of everyday life. It was not a custom they invented. A little hard liquor to warm the innards in frigid winter weather had been eastern Europe's contribution to Judaism. And if the Christians did not spiritualize their drinking as the Jews had done, they drank at least as heavily. The Hasidim with characteristic zest had merely taken up the general custom, adding to it, in honor of the Baal Shem Tov's pipe, a little ritualistic smoking. And though the brothers consumed no more than the others—just a pleasant buzz, a send-off to holy intoxication—they enjoyed it more; to sobersides, enjoyment is a great scandal.

It would be wrong to imagine that the poor Hasidim, the peasants and villagers, were entirely the innocent victims of the secularization of the zaddik's court. It had been a mutual process of corruption. Their own vanity had been puffed up by their leader's riches. Their pride in themselves increased correspondingly their awe of him. By reacting over the generations with more enthusiasm for their leaders' materialistic display than for their spiritual characteristics, they had encouraged the human weaknesses of their zaddikim. And, as the zaddikim have warned again and again in every generation, they are and must be subject to human weaknesses.

Instead of laughing at their foolishness, their followers encouraged grander displays and fierce rivalries among the zaddikim. They repeated and magnified idle words, fanning anger, joining in the resultant fray with tongues wagging and scurrilous pens. By the end of the nineteenth century, at least a dozen Hasid courts behaved toward each other like nations at war. Propaganda, much of it coldly slanderous lies, poured through the Hasidic world in shock waves and counter-shock waves of hostility. At times words alone could not contain the aroused fury. Hotheads from rival brotherhoods—hoodlum gangs carrying weapons—invaded each other's territory in surprise attacks resulting in bloodshed and death. More than once the entire Jewish community in a given locality was shamed by the necessity of calling in gentile police to control their battling Hasidim. And more than once the Jewish community was abjectly shamed and shocked when quarreling brotherhoods conspired with governmental agents to arrest and imprison their own.

The office of zaddik had become hedged with formalities and ritual. Often humble, unworldly, peaceful zaddikim, wanting no part of the court's ostentation and rivalry, were the puppets of ruthless, purse-proud disciples who ground out the meaningless displays of pomp and strategies of terror around their bewildered and forlorn persons.

This pattern is common to every historic religious movement. The essence of the problem seems to be that humanity is made of such dull and heavy stuff that the leavening power of our prophets and holy men is soon spent and, though it works its miracle on individuals, humanity works its suffocating effect on the movement. And then again saints like leaves on a tree come in different gradations. Some seem to have more power than others; perhaps it is more sparks of the holy Shekhinah. Whatever the cause, the power of the man can be measured by the leavening effect he has on humanity around him. And great ones like the Besht are sadly rare.

Nevertheless, the great ones do leave more behind than a movement that slowly becomes weighed down by human folly and vindictiveness. They leave a record of their methods. And these methods can be taken up and used even while the movement wavers. They leave behind them memories— the story of their lives. And these stories contain heartbeats of their person, pulses of power that can motivate and energize spiritual progress.

10

The Whirlwind with a Glib Tongue

THE EVILS OF corrupt zaddikism loom hideous relative to the mystical illumination that radiated from the presence of the Baal Shem Tov and the other Hasidic holy men. They had the power to evoke spiritual awakening in those who touched them. Their lives, their beings were their prime torah. God and the care of his people was their prime ambition. Against the backdrop of their times the nineteenth-century zaddikim were no different from other clergy of their times. A few were totally corrupt. Most were good men entangled in a role beyond their capacities. But even in this period of decadence, where the man fit the role, his community and all who came in contact with him were transformed.

Herein lies the hidden moral of the life of Rabbi Nachman of Bratslav.

Chronologically he belongs at the beginning of the period we have just finished discussing rather than at its end. But what the man was doing can only be understood in terms of the currents that had begun in his lifetime, currents whose inevitable course he perceived clearly.

The great-grandchild of the Baal Shem Tov, Nachman ben Ssimha could have floated to power and glory among the Hasidim with token effort. Instead he sought God with the wild insistence of a Kabbalistic mystic. Without a trustworthy master to guide his progress, his impatient rush accomplished little more than ruined health and misery.

Just as his great-grandfather had been appalled by the rabbis of his day, young Nachman looked at the ostentation and pretense of the Hasidic court with angry, hurt eyes. Rejecting all things Hasidic, including the Besht's proscription of bodily penance, Nachman applied himself to the terrible Lurianic austerities. His boyhood became a rhythm of prolonged fasting followed by spurts of gobbling down, unenjoyed, just enough food to keep himself alive. In marathon efforts to batter down the obstacles between himself and God, he prayed at the Besht's grave under the blistering summer sun and through sleepless winter nights of blustering cold—and failed to accomplish his purpose. Even that moment of agony when he broke the ice to plunge his skinny body into the frigid water of the ritual bath each winter day accomplished no more than to set his bones to an aching that became as much a part of him as ground-in dirt became part of a peasant's hands.

He could not seem to touch even the shadow of God. His soul felt as heavy as clay. Depression weighed him down. His only relief came in tears and those only after long bouts of frustrated effort.

The Hasidic community, his marriage at fourteen, the expectations of his elders seemed blocks in his way. He could not move them or circumvent them. Indirectly, however, his marriage did contain his path. According to the custom, he settled in the village of his father-in-law. Outside the blotch of huts and houses and farm fields, he discovered the same guide his great-grandfather had had in the Carpathian Mountains: Nature. A city boy, his only previous glimpses of its workings were in the crippled growth in isolated, empty lots. But there in the forest edging into the village, a horse, his only companion, he saw the rhythms and power of Nature. Day after day he climbed up wooded slopes and investigated narrow ravines. Physical activity strengthened his body and the aloneness with natural cycles and unperverted instincts opened his soul. As they had to his great-grandfather, growing things began to talk to him. They spoke of God. Each plant that pushed its way through the soil, each bud bursting into color seemed to sing of the glory of life and thankfulness for being part of God.

At last his heart learned the Hasidic torah that God is in all things. The revelation infused him with the desire to show others what he had seen. He settled down in a small town and began moving among the people, urging them to prepare themselves to see God, who is present everywhere if only they would learn how to look.

But as he praised God, he rejected zaddikism. As his great-grandfather had scoffed and raged at the rabbis, Nachman stormed and vilified the vain, grasping, exclusive office-holders and figureheads who sat on the thrones of Hasidic dynasties. Everywhere he went, his enthusiasm and devotion to God won him followers. A group began forming around him. But his accomplishments seemed pitifully inadequate in his own eyes compared to the task he had set himself: drying up the mire of corruption into which the Hasidic world was sinking. He felt the need for a powerful mystic force to energize his mission. Intuitively he felt that a pilgrimage to the Holy Land would supply that impetus. Blandly he announced his decision to go. His followers and family would have been little more astounded if he had told them he was leaving for the moon.

For years his family and he had been struggling along on the tiny income his father-in-law gave them. Eventually financial disaster had dried up that trickle of revenue. To keep the Nachman family alive, his followers scraped together such coins as they could spare. When finding food was such a daily problem, how could he find money for such an expensive trip?

And suppose he succeeded in making his way to the Holy Land, what would happen to his wife and children while he was away? Who would feed them? Even his followers thought the trip was a rash idea. His wife begged him not to leave. He ignored her. She sent their daughter to plead for the family. He ignored his daughter, too. Nachman was indifferent to everything but his vision of Israel. He told his wife and the older children that they would have to hire themselves out as servants. The younger children should be placed in the homes of anyone willing to take them. And the money for the trip he found by selling all of his family's possessions.

Accompanied by only one disciple, he made his way to the port city of Odessa in southern Russia. From there he went by boat through stormy seas to Constantinople. It is not too surprising that he was suspected by the Turkish officials of being a French spy; those were the days of Napoleon when everyone was feeling jittery. But Nachman had forbidden his disciple to give out the least hint of his identity, so he was cold-shouldered and even abused by the city's Jews.

From his point of view the Turks had been fortuitous. The Jews' rejection he had planned himself. Self-inflicted humiliation was another penance. It almost seems as if he viewed it as a trade with God: if he had not suffered in Constantinople, he never would have reached Israel. He added such other touches as he could manage, walking about barefooted and, except for the necessary yarmulke, bare-headed. No doubt he would have loved also to go without food, but the necessity of conserving his strength forced him to eat a little.

When he finally was able to find a boat bound for Palestine whose fare he could afford, he had had physical duress enough to suit even him, but the seas were rough, and the boat rolled in the waves. Nachman was seized with seasickness of the violent and long-lasting sort. During the bad weather the ship's captain managed to sail in among the French fleet and for a time the French seriously considered sinking or capturing the alien boat.

The suffering came to an end on the eve of Rosh Hashanah when the ship docked at Haifa. Nachman's need for disguising his identity was over. Word of his arrival traveled fast—the great-grandson of the Besht! The Hasidic brotherhood in Palestine opened their arms to him.

Nachman's trip to the Holy Land can be compared with a Bar Mitzvah boy's visit to his zaddik. In a real sense Palestine functioned as a zaddik for him. He himself acknowledged Palestine as the headwaters of his piety and wisdom as he never acknowledged indebtedness to a human source, not even his great-grandfather. Many times he told his disciples in later years that whatever holiness he possessed came as a result of his having lived in Palestine.

The mystical quickening was immediate and deep. He became overwhelmed with emotion, intoxicated with devotion to God and joy at walking on the soil of the prophets. Often during his stay, he was incapable of speech. His throat could not squeeze out the words. He moved about dazed and distracted, his attention focused on the spiritual plane. Despite pleas from the Palestine Hasidim, he shied away from honors and requests to give his torah and discuss holy matters. At times the intensity of his emotions threatened to require for his health's sake that he leave the Holy Land prematurely.

Faced with the threat of having to depart, he forced his joy back to such levels as his body could tolerate. In the end it was the obligation he felt to his disciples that brought him home. He returned carrying the memory of Palestine in his heart and the intimacy with God which he acquired there radiating from his being.

To his disciples it seemed he came back to them a veritable Angel of God, ecstatically proclaiming His truths to the brotherhood while searing the ears of the unrighteous zaddikim with words of flame. Suggesting they were in fact servants of Satan, his attacks on them became so merciless and telling that the zaddikim began to believe Nachman was a threat to their positions. Politically, they were well established in the community, buttressed by large accumulations of wealth and by deeply entrenched channels of power. The warring dynasties united at least in their hatred of Nachman, charging him with treachery to the cause of Hasidism and denouncing his teachings as dangerous and radical. Eventually the zaddikim were able to bring down upon him the same nightmare of isolation that the rabbis had inflicted upon the Hasidim. He and his brotherhood were forbidden the use of the synagogues, any secular commerce, and social contact.

For himself Nachman enjoyed penance, but he could not allow himself to be the cause of his disciples' suffering. As others had done before him, he left the community that had been his home and the birthplace of his brotherhood and settled in Bratslav.

The people of Bratslav regarded Hasidic doctrines with approval. However, the town had no dynastic court or even a well organized brotherhood. They were pleased to have a holy man come among them.

Quickly the young people gathered around the new teacher, listening to his torah and soaking up his devotion to God until it became their own. Nachman was a tender master. He stepped between his followers and their fears, their doubts, and even their sins. He urged them to make a beginning from where they were at that moment: not to look behind at what they had done or what they had been, but to look forward to God. He would do their penance for them. He would rebuild all that they had harmed. They need only love God and have confidence to continue moving forward in their spiritual exercises.

When he was among his followers, they were the greater part of his daily life. And when he went traveling across the country to find new followers, he wrote frequently to those he had to leave behind, assuring them of their place in his heart. Teaching was not the only purpose of his travels. Since his visit to Palestine, he had discovered that his presence had a mystical effect on those around him. He had acquired the ability to free men's spirits from the tangle of materialism so that they were able to feel desire for God.

He spoke to the peasants as his great-grandfather had, telling them not to worry about abstruse arguments and subtle doctrines but to believe that each step forward they took created an angel that raised them higher toward God. Without pomp and display, he entered the village squares and transformed the lives of those he met.

Ironically, he had become a zaddik. He had attacked zaddikism and still was attacking it. But as a zaddik, he was discovering the realities of the role. He was discovering that the same characteristic can have two effects depending on the presence or absence of intangibles. He saw that those who loved him and served him *were* sanctified. And he found himself recommending the single-minded adoration that true holy men and frauds have advocated since time immemorial. "Eat or do not eat," he told his disciples. "Sleep or do not sleep, pray or do not pray, but come to me."

It was an awkward position and one his enemies did not fail to attack, accusing him of self-interested hypocrisy. The attacks were launched but they never seemed to touch Nachman. When his disciples became indignant over the accusations, he tried to soothe their anger, explaining to them that it was not really he the zaddikim were attacking but a straw man they had formed out of their own ignorance.

As his powers ripened, his compassion grew and sweetened. His dislike of materialism was as great as ever, making him struggle unceasingly to lift his disciples above that plane. Materialists, he told them, were slaves to their desires and always in debt to their ambitions whereas the truly holy person turns away from the competition for wealth.

To the poor, in place of wealth, Nachman tried to give his love of Nature. Wealth was a habit that became increasingly vicious. Nature is a guide and nourisher, but to Nachman, Nature had one other capacity as well: Nature was a temple of worship. Out under the sky in the sweet-smelling air, a person's prayers become impregnated with the music of the flowers and grasses, and from their blissful melodies, prayers gain the power to soar to heaven.

Despite the harsh truths he proclaimed about the zaddikim, when he was among the poor and the powerless, he found endless reasons to overlook human failings. He encouraged the liar to speak truthfully, the spiteful man to be tender, and the boastful man to be more humble; but he never bullied or threatened. Instead he assured his followers that the weakest among them had sufficient divine sparks within him to take him up to God.

As his sweetness grew so did the savor of his torah. The illumination he received in Palestine glowed with a brighter incandescence by the month. He perceived the necessity of presenting his teachings in a form that would delight as well as instruct. He had to capture his listener's interest before he could teach him. He preached less; instead, like his great-grandfather, he began to teach by means of parables and stories.

Nachman was not a writer. He was one of the last of the great Jewish storytellers. He became consummate in its skills. He learned to take time in developing his themes, building up suspense in his audience. Often his listeners would beg him to finish a tale, but he would smile and shake his head. He teased them along, knowing the game kept their thoughts directed toward God. For this reason, many of his stories, like the Tale of the Clever Man and the Simple Man, wind their way through details and detours with charming elaborations to make a moral that a logician would write in a sentence or two. For many of Nachman's tales, we can give thanks to the thorough notes of his disciple Natham of Nemerov. He took to copying down the tales so that he could share them with those who were not, at the time, fortunate enough to be at Nachman's side.

Natham was a perfect example of the devotion to the zaddik that transforms a disciple's character and heart. He placed himself completely at his master's disposal, and step by step his love led him to greatness he would not have accomplished on his own.

Transcribing Nachman's tales was a little like transcribing jazz: Natham could capture one version of a tale but not all the wonderful, subtle variations that occurred with each telling. Still, one version of many is better than none. Natham's coming—he did not meet Nachman until 1802—was fortuitous.

Almost from birth Nachman had flagrantly burned his energies as though they were a Sabbath candle to be sacrificed. By the time that Natham became a disciple, the flame of Nachman's physical energies had begun to flicker. Tubercle bacilli had gained entry to his system and had not been repelled. He may have taken one icy bath too many. Chronic exhaustion and time had allowed the disease to consume his lungs. For years he had kept his sickness from his disciples, but when bright red blood came from his hemorrhaging lungs, concealment was no longer possible. Eventually, any prolonged speech started the bleeding again.

When his master was no longer able to travel across the countryside, Natham became his body, walking the long routes, telling and retelling Nachman's stories, recounting his experiences with his master, and preaching Nachman's teachings. It seemed to Natham he could not walk far enough, could not talk long enough or loud enough to carry the message out over the land. He began to gather money together so that the stories he had written down could be published and reach those places his feet could not travel. It took years of saving, but finally he bought his own printing press which he set up in Bratslav to give his master a voice that could not sicken.

Nachman was only thirty-nine and he was dying. Yet the knowledge of forthcoming death filled him with a sense of relief. He had left Palestine and returned to Poland to lead his people and give them comfort and truth. Shortly before he died he told his disciples, I live only by the fact that I was in the Holy Land. To him death was freedom to travel to a holier land. It was a gift.

He did not die in Bratslav, the town he had made famous with his life. The year before the end, he began searching for a place where he could fulfill his mission as a zaddik even in the act of dying. At last he found what he was looking for—Uman—the place where Jews by the hundreds had been slaughtered in 1648. He wanted to be buried near those martyrs so that those who had been unable to enter heaven might at last enter it with him. During the last days, when he saw his disciples weeping, he hushed them, promising to prepare a place for them, smiling like a homesick boy returning home.

Even at the last, however, his love for his followers was a bond that could not be broken. He promised Natham that he was not leaving his disciples. Natham and the others held him to that promise, building a synagogue near Nachman's grave and pilgrimaging by the hundreds to seek his help as they had when he was alive.

The Rav

11

AT THE MOMENT there are a number of Hasidic brother-hoods in the continental United States.

The followers of the zaddikim of Skver have established an entire township, New Square, in Rockland County, New York. New Square is a bit of eastern Europe of the past situated near ultra-urban New York City; it maintains its old customs and traditions. Following World War II, the zad-dikim and many of their followers of several Hungarian dynasties immigrated to this country, settling for the most part in adjoining neighborhoods in New York City and Brooklyn and trying to continue as if war and time had not interfered with the operations of their customs.

The mysticism of these dynasties along with their sepa-rate traditions and the differing emphases of their teachings have survived the new environment. But what they have to offer is given only to themselves. Newcomers, even within the Jewish faith, are looked upon with suspicion. Leadership and congregation membership within the brotherhoods are hereditary. Eventually, their accomplishments may be writ-ten up and made available to a larger public, but for the moment, essentially they are hidden mystics, and we can benefit only indirectly from their existence.

There is, however, in America and elsewhere, on Hasidic dynasty that has opened itself to public view, that is international in scope, and that is actively recruiting membership.

A strong, exciting movement from its beginnings, Chabad Hasidism today is potent and energetic—in America at least, *the* dynamic movement of contemporary Hasidism. Unlike the other divergent schools of the original Hasidism, Chabad has reached out into the world's Jewish community, maintaining a nonexclusionary presence, and making itself available as a center of youthful energy. Nonpracticing Jews raised outside the Hasidic tradition are eagerly welcomed into Chabad. If they wish, they will be shown, through study and tutoring, the Chabad Way.

Chabad means systematic thought. The word is actually an acrostic of three Hebrew words: *chochma, binah,* and *daat.* These words denote three types of knowledge. Chochma is the concept, binah is the development, and daat is the culmination of knowledge.

Chabad works in the following way: In the attempt to comprehend a subject, very often a flash of illumination strikes the mind. It may be just a spark, but that spark holds the germ of the solution. Left alone and undeveloped, this germ might be lost. The germ is like a point in geometry, possessing but one dimension—a beginning. This beginning is chochma, the nucleus of the concept, the genesis of intellectual activity, the moment of creation. Binah adds dimension, examining and developing the chochma or nucleus in detail and implication. Although the concept is changed in the process, it is replaced by comprehension. Daat, the conclusion, is made possible by concentration and dedication to the intellectual process. Different conclusions for different problems—including the stimulation of appropriate emotions—all come under the process of daat. The Chabad Hasidim believe that with the proper application of the three processes of chochma, binah, and daat, one can control and alter radically his emotions and his actions.

The orginator of this discipline and the founder of Chabad Hasidism was Shneur Zalman, known by his followers as the Rav, the teacher, Dov Baer's favorite disciple.

In this country we have a heritage of putting what we can in a bag or wagon or car and taking off into the unknown in search of better opportunities. Shneur Zalman's family had the same tradition except that they were looking for a more promising spiritual environment. And, as if to underline the difference, they moved eastward rather than westward; a series of moves stretched over three generations brought the family to Liozna, a town close to Lubavitch, for generations into the misty past the home of hidden Jewish mystics.

Lubavitch was a small town; when Shneur Zalman was growing up, it had seventy-five or so Jewish families, a square-mile clump of humanity surrounded by wild, deep forest and bordered by two rivers. Largely isolated from the nightmare of Europe, Lubavitch was its own world, a world of saints who looked like farmers, small artisans, and shopkeepers, because they worked at those jobs and loved their work as they loved each other and their life and God, who gave all of these things meaning for them.

The town was founded, no one knows when, by six Jewish families in search of a place where they might live "on the land," earning and eating by their own labor in harmony with Nature. The acts of kindness by the cooperative's leader, a man named Meir, are remembered to this day in stories and fable. The town was named for the atmosphere he created; Lubavitch, the Town of Brotherly Love. It was really a part of the forest. The chittering of squirrels and bird calls were as much a part of its daily sounds as the rise and fall of human conversation. The air of Lubavitch buzzed and sparked with mysticism and its people had holy eyes.

Young Shneur Zalman may have breathed in mysticism when he visited Lubavitch to study with his teacher, but his abilities and interest as a child were directed toward scholarship. The child prodigy is a tradition in Jewish religious biography, but the evidence suggests that Shneur Zalman was one of those who gave the tradition substance. His elders thought him a genius, referring to him as an *iluy*, an exalted one, the title bestowed on the cream of the young scholars.

When he was Bar Mitzvah, he was taken in as a member of the *Hebrah Kaddishah*, a hidden mystical brotherhood that operated under the front of being a nursing and mortuary organization. And at that time his name on the town record was accorded the title rabbi, a rare honor even for an iluy.

Two years later the young rabbi was married to the daughter of a wealthy man who wanted a respected scholar and successful rabbi in his family. A scholar he got, but not the use of the scholar. According to the custom, Shneur Zalman did come to live with his wife's parents; but instead of finding himself a place in the synagogue and reaping profitable rewards from his years of study, he continued night and day at his books until his father-in-law, irate and no doubt desperate, refused to give him candles or lamps. It was a blow. It was a hindrance. But on the nights when the moon shone, Shneur Zalman studied, and he continued to refuse to put his studying to practical use.

By the time he was twenty, he felt he had done all he could in the house of his father-in-law. He had read and reread and absorbed the Talmud, its commentaries, and the books of the Kabbalah. To progress further, he needed a master. The logical and prestigious choice was Elijah, the Gaon of Wilna.

Then he heard rumors of Dov Baer.

He knew what Elijah had to offer him. It was an extension of what he had already learned. It was the perfection of the methods he had already used.

But the Maggid was a question mark.

To the horror and utter despair of his father-in-law, the question mark won. He set off for Meseritz.

What his father-in-law said at their parting is not recorded. It is known that Shneur Zalman traveled without funds, earning his way as he went by odd jobs such as chopping wood and doing farm work. Traveling like that is slow going. When at last he arrived in Meseritz and made his way to the Maggid's court, he felt it had all been wasted effort. The scene with his father-in-law, his wife's tears, his bruised muscles and empty stomach—all had been for nothing, a mistake in judgment. The court was tawdry; Dov Baer's torah seemed to him silly prattle.

Then the Maggid caught his eye. The Maggid had been taught occult techniques by the Besht. He may have known someone he needed was coming toward him. Or he may have read Shneur Zalman's character and his destiny in that look. Whichever, he decided he wanted the young man as his disciple. Shneur Zalman felt the Maggid's eyes boring into his. They seemed to go through the flesh, reaching, probing and testing his soul, its dimensions and quality. Then, before Shneur Zalman could say a word, Dov Baer read his mind. He had found in that searching gaze the two test questions the young man had planned to ask in the hope of assessing his potential master's abilities. Dov Baer stated the questions and answered them in a way that filled the young scholar with wonder.

That look and those questions changed the hard-headed intellectual into a mystic and doting follower of the Maggid's. The capacity had been there all the time, developed through the mind's way of learning without knowing it knows, in the heady atmosphere of Lubavitch. Dov Baer had removed the barrier to his use of it.

To the new convert it was a miracle. For years he had been oppressed with an inner dryness and fatigue that choked his being. They were gone, replaced by joy and exuberance. His hesitancy and self-doubts had vanished. Confidence, decisiveness, and assurance pulsed through him. No wonder he adored the Maggid, commenting in his diary that in the house of his teacher we drew up the Shekhinah by the bucketful and miracles lay around under the benches, only no one had time to pick them up.

The disciple quickly became a teacher for the Maggid's son Abraham, nicknamed Malach—Angel—because he acted like one. And the teacher openly acknowledged that he learned as much as he gave. Through Malach's eyes he saw a Dov Baer that few knew. It was the beginning of an intimacy new to him and one that he needed. His father-in-law might have had that closeness but for the man's greed. In Shneur Zalman's response to the relationship, one sees the immensity of loyalty and devotion of which his father-in-law robbed himself. He had one more chance when Shneur Zalman returned home at the end of a year and a half to retrieve his promise. But the father-in-law ruined that opportunity, too; or perhaps it had been lost in that first look between Shneur Zalman and the Maggid. The facts are that after a short stay, the young disciple hurried back to court and stayed with his master until death.

For his part, though not a sentimental man, Dov Baer took to gloating openly about his wonder-disciple—an occupation that did nothing for Shneur Zalman's relationships with his brother disciples. In addition to the recognition he gave him, Dov Baer kept him occupied with tasks that made the most of and demanded more of Shneur Zalman's abilities.

One of the most awesome of those duties was the assignment of rewriting and integrating Rabbi Joseph Cairo's *Sulchan Aruch*—The Code of Jewish Law—and its two-hundred-year addendum of commentaries, glossaries, and critical notes. He spent more than three years absorbing and untangling the morass of written judgment and opinion. His own writing was a sporadic effort over the years whenever his other duties permitted; and before it could be published, fire consumed some of the finished manuscript. But no matter, the result, filling five volumes, was masterly. Not only had he condensed and integrated the library of rabbinical decisions, he had included in his version short explanations and indications of the sources for each decision, an advantage that Cairo's code lacked and one that has made Shneur Zalman's code a standard reference work with orthodox rabbis as well as with the Hasidim.

Earlier, we met and saw Shneur Zalman in action during the crisis following his master's death. From the moment of Dov Baer's dying until his own death, most of the joy of Shneur Zalman's life came from within. The man who had converted two czars of Russia to a belief in his innocence and in the essential goodness of Hasidism, the scholar who at twenty-five was rewriting Jewish law, the Hasid whose name was being praised by the orthodox for his pious behavior during imprisonment, was disliked if not hated by his brother disciples.

The Maggid's abundant praise of his disciple had sown bitter seed. However, the matter may have gone deeper than jealousy. Shneur Zalman's personality stood out among most of his brother disciples like an owl among nightingales. Mystics, men of passionate emotion, distrustful of the intellect, believed his personality to be more an obstacle and a source of false pride than a serviceable tool. Shneur Zalman was their mirror image. He was just as mystical, just as devoted to God and the Maggid, but he was as distrustful of raw emotion in every other regard as they were of intellect.

Suspicion, irritation, and misunderstanding between the other disciples and Shneur Zalman may have been inevitable. His brother disciples had been, of course, pleased when he deferred to Menahem Mendel on the matter of leadership. However, they could not be unaware that the older man had in the main given Shneur Zalman the functions of leadership and the entire role, title and all, on the occasion of Menahem Mendel's move to the Holy Land.

One wonders if the letters Shneur Zalman wrote during the crisis with Elijah, the Gaon of Wilna, begging for cool heads and compassionate hearts did not instead serve to keep warm and smoldering his brother disciples' irritation at him. It was there, ready to flare over his dispute with Abraham of Kalish, the leader of the brotherhood in the Holy Land. Abraham, another disciple of the Maggid and a man of great heart but a poor sense of organization, administered the monies sent to him for the maintenance of the conventicle in the Holy Land. Shneur Zalman, who had spent much time and energy raising funds for this project, was dismayed at the lackadaisical way they were handled and suggested to Abraham that he be more careful in his management and provide an accounting.

The request outraged Abraham, who felt it was a direct challenge to his integrity. He appealed to his fellow zaddikim, sparking the tensions and hostilities that had been accumulating over the years. Charges and vituperation came crashing down on Shneur Zalman, lightly touching on the matter of Abraham and his funds, but concentrating most of their intensity on Shneur Zalman's new approach to Hasidism, which we will explore carefully. Not only was his methodology damned but his person was denounced as lacking character, devotion to God, and loyalty to the Hasidic cause.

Now that it was his person that bore the brunt of Hasidic rage, Shneur Zalman maintained the same stance as he had when his brothers were denouncing Elijah, the Gaon. The grief Shneur Zalman must have felt he kept to himself, doing all that he could to soothe his brothers' feelings and to awaken in them the sense that they *were* all brothers, all disciples of the Maggid, working toward the same goal in their own individual ways.

At best he was only partially successful. The zaddikim's fury would subside, only to surge up again over something he did or said.

One such instance occurred in 1805, when the Russian government had belched one of its periodic persecutions of Jews, ousting thousands of Jews from its villages, denying the rights of the Jews to own inns and taverns, confiscating valuable property. Shneur Zalman left home and began traveling across Poland, collecting money for the dispossessed and exiled. When he arrived in Medziboz, the Besht's grandson Barukh denounced Shneur Zalman for encroaching upon his private preserve. When Shneur Zalman pleaded the cause of the starving Russian Jews, Barukh told him coldly, "What business is it of yours? Let them die!"

But Shneur Zalman believed that benevolence—*zeddakah*—had the same spiritual value as prayer. He was as deeply committed to service to the people as were Elimelech and Jacob Isaac the Seer. Only their methodologies differed; Shneur Zalman believed in dealing with materialistic problems on a materialistic level, not through occult manipulation. In his brotherhood he made social service a prime duty, stating that zeddakah, like a magnet, draws out divine influence. The Shekhinah reveals itself in benevolence, taking away man's sin, restoring him to innocence. Benevolence, he said many times, is the best way of combating evil thoughts.

He himself practiced zeddakah all his life. There seemed always a cause he was working to further, gathering funds, spending time, exerting influence. One of his favorite causes was the relocation of ghetto Jews to farmland of their own. His experience in Lubavitch had convinced him that working the land was better for the soul than grubbing for a livelihood in the stench and corruption of city life.

He had begun to develop a new philosophy of Hasidism and to put it into practice in the White Russian brotherhood that had formed around him after Menahem Mendel left for the Holy Land. His leadership of the brotherhood and the development of his ideas took place at the same time he was engaged in his social work. From his point of view it was all one commitment with many facets. For his followers, he discouraged if not actually prohibited the use of the occult. And, though he was the zaddik of the brotherhood in White Russia, he refused its title, insisting that his disciples call him Rav—teacher—or *Alter Rebbe*—the old Rebbe—as they did in later years. The worship of his person he did his very best to discourage, feeling that this aspect of zaddikism led to corruption.

His rejection of zaddikism was not a rejection of the Besht or Dov Baer, but a recognition of the reality that such men are rare, too rare to design an organization around on the assumption that in each generation such holy men will be found. The petty bickerings of his brother zaddikim had convinced him that the theory of zaddikism does not always work out in the flesh because the lesser saints are flecked through with human frailty.

Shneur Zalman acknowledged that through the grace of God such great ones come from time to time, but these were exceptional beings; their holiness was inborn. When these great ones came, great things were accomplished and mankind was blessed. For those times no planning was needed.

Shneur Zalman planned his brotherhood for the other times when the community must struggle along without a great one, when the *beinoni*—the average human being—must take over the work of serving God. Shneur Zalman believed that the beinoni, though he lacked the inborn holiness of a Besht, can strive for perfection. He cannot achieve complete integration with God in his lifetime, but by discipline and perseverance, he can fulfill his own potential.

In addition to zeddakah Shneur Zalman urged his brotherhood to meditate on the greatness of the Creator and to cultivate a joyful love of God that prevents melancholy. Characteristically, he toned down the Hasidic demonstrativeness at prayer, feeling that too much elation led to an easy thrill rather than to the sustaining love that comes from study and thoughtfulness. Discipline was his central theme. Daily regular study, punctual observation of the times of prayer. The logical development of thought that gave Chabad Hasidism its name. He believed the intellect was strengthened by studying the Torah, and faith was strengthened by studying the Kabbalah. This disciplined approach could arouse love of God, but not, in his opinion, comprehension of Him.

Shneur Zalman believed that for man on this plane there is an unbridgeable gap between the inconceivable power and divine essence of God, and man. He felt any attempt on the part of normal human consciousness to understand or to imagine or to identify That which is God is bound to fall short of its goal. Since man cannot know God or understand God or anticipate God, he had best surrender his being to that unknown, joyfully accepting God's will and discovering that will by studying the Torah and the other revelations that God has given to man.

This philosophic foundation of Chabad Hasidism was an elaboration that Shneur Zalman made of discussions he had had with Dov Baer. Chabad breaks in many instances with the Hasidic method, though its essence is Hasidic and comes in a direct line from his discipleship to Dov Baer and Dov Baer's to the Besht.

To Shneur Zalman the two facts about God, which man must recognize, are His omniscience and His omnipotence. From these facts it follows that every single aspect of creation is under God's direct supervision. Unlike many of his contemporaries, he did not believe and could not believe in creation as a single act that then proceeded to unfold mechanically: creation is, not creation was. Nothing is possible or can take place without God's knowledge and will. Every leaf that blows or gnat that buzzes or pebble that rolls down a talus slide is being witnessed by God and is part of his design. We exist because God holds us in his mind. If he stopped for a microsecond, we would cease to exist. If we are in God, at the same time, God is everywhere in his creation. There is no particle too small to hold God or space so empty that it is not filled with God's presence or object so vile that its essential being is not God's Holy Person. Shneur Zalman quotes the Holy Scripture: "Do I not fill the heavens and earth, says the Lord."

Shneur Zalman's concept of evil is more reminiscent of that of the writer of the Book of Job than of the Besht. Shneur Zalman believed that evil is absolute. It exists through the will of God and therefore its overall function is good. But insofar as man is concerned, evil is absolutely evil and was created to test human goodness. If evil were relative, the test would not be valid. He illustrates his theory with a story of a king who hired a hussy to test his son's virtue, telling the woman to use all her arts and wiles on the boy to see if she could seduce him. For the king's purpose the test had to be real to accomplish his aim, and for God's purpose evil must be real.

Because Shneur Zalman was a prolific writer, we have abundant first-person testaments to his ideas. One of his most famous books on metaphysical speculation is a collection of short articles and letters called *Tanya*. This anthology focuses on the search for God, the ultimate reality in Whom all things have their being. Heaven as a paradise held no interest for Shneur Zalman. His search was for God Himself. His desire was to return to and be absorbed in God.

The Rav's last brush with social work came as a result of Napoleon's invasion of Russia. His reaction to Napoleon and the invasion was typical of the man.

Among the emperor's virtues was an absence of the religious prejudice that characterized most Europeans of his time. He had left behind in the wake of his conquests the Code of Napoleon. So when he promised the Russian Jews freedom from harassment and the rights of citizenship and human dignity, they had only to look to France, Spain, and Germany to see that Napoleon's promises were true predictions of future policy.

From the czars the Jews knew what to expect: crushing taxation, segregation, discrimination, persecution, and periodically, expulsion, violence, and mass murder. Needless to say, most of the European Jews including the Hasidic zaddikim leaned heavily toward Napoleon.

Not so Shneur Zalman.

He looked not at how Napoleon treated the Jews but at the kind of environment he created where he ruled. And the Rav saw raw materialism and the drive for power rather than for God. And the Rav became afraid. He knew a victory for Napoleon in Russia would improve the lot of Jews materialistically, but he feared the subtle erosion of their religious life.

Shneur Zalman rallied the Russian Jews to the czarist cause. Although Jews fought in neither army, the line of battle and the terrible winter of occupation occurred in areas heavily populated by Jews. Their allegiance importantly affected the final outcome of the fighting. How important that allegiance was can be estimated from the gratitude the czar and his government showed to the family of Shneur Zalman. Gratitude from the czar to a Jew did not come easily.

The city of Ladi, which had been Shneur Zalman's headquarters for some time, stood directly in the path of Napoleon's victorious sweep to Moscow. The Rav stood between his people and panic and never despaired of the final outcome, predicting that Napoleon would reach the capital and waste his strength there. Just as Laydy's last defenses were collapsing, he took his family and made a dash to get beyond Napoleon's reach, declaring he would rather die escaping than live under the emperor's rule.

Shneur Zalman's declaration was a prophecy. Exhaustion, overwork, and exposure weakened him, and he became too sick to travel farther. A Russian peasant took him into his hut to provide him with shelter, but the village lacked a doctor and the medical supplies Shneur Zalman needed.

He died in the last month of 1812.

Chabad: The Average Man's Path to God

IN THE WAKE of his father's death, Shneur Zalman's son and successor was presented with a rare opportunity. Shneur Zalman's mobilization of the Russian Jews against Napoleon had struck a telling and perhaps crucial blow to Napoleon's army of occupation.

On hearing of Shneur Zalman's death, the minister of war called the cabinet together for the sole purpose of sending a joint message of sympathy to the grieving family. Czar Alexander I conferred on the son, whom Shneur Zalman had named after his beloved teacher, the hereditary title, Honored Citizen. And more importantly, the honors were accompanied by an inquiry as to how the government could best show its gratitude to Shneur Zalman's heir.

Rabbi Dov Baer could think of no better way than in fulfilling his father's dream to settle Jews on farmland of their own. A program instigated by the czarist government and administered in large part through the Chabad brotherhood brought thousands of Jewish familes to a new life in Kherson. Rabbi Dov Baer exploited this opportunity to the fullest, exerting continued pressure on the government for better treatment of the Jewish community and urging the community to develop the farm techniques and other manual skills that would result in their becoming more economically effective.

It is not surprising that the Rav's brotherhood led by his son should adopt a continuing interest and involvement in social work, but the organized program that has come to be typical of Chabad activity had its beginnings at this time. It is part of Chabad belief that efforts in social welfare are actually part of its program to develop spiritual awareness; the belief is supported by a saying of the Besht's: A hole in the body makes a larger hole in the soul.

Rabbi Dov Baer's selection of the future home for the sorrowing brotherhood was superb: Lubavitch, the forest home of mystics where his father had studied as a boy. The Town of Brotherly Love with its three main streets and the old marketplace bustling at the heart of the village was much the same as in his father's boyhood, although the number of Jewish families had grown to one hundred ten.

The brotherhood sank long roots in Lubavitch, drawing spiritual sustenance from the atmosphere. When they went forth from Lubavitch, the Chabad Hasidim tried to take part of Lubavitch with them. To this day they speak of establishing an "environment." And although the Communists drove them from their hundred-year home, the leaders of Chabad still refer to themselves as the Lubavitcher rebbes—learned persons—just as in memory of their founder they also call themselves the *Schneersohn*—son of Shneur—dynasty.

Rabbi Dov Baer was succeeded by his brother-in-law, Menahem Mendel of Lubavitch, who was also the grandson of Shneur Zalman, and who, due to the early death of his parents, was largely raised and educated by his grandfather. He was succeeded by his youngest son Samuel, who was succeeded by his son Sholom Dov Baer, famous as the founder of the first *yeshivah*—religious school which can produce rabbis—marking the organized beginnings of religious education in the Chabad movement.

His son Joseph Isaac Schneersohn was born to make things happen and to have things happen to.

Joseph Isaac was fifteen when his father made him his

personal secretary and emissary to international religious convocations and important political-diplomatic missions to improve the social condition of Russian Jews. After generations of casting a benevolent eye upon the Schneersohn family, the czarist government, shortly after World War I, was again scapegoating Jews to take its subjects' minds off their grating poverty. Joseph Isaac Schneersohn was jailed four times by the czarist government for fighting for Jewish rights.

When the revolution struck, he was in the thick of organizing medical help for the injured and food supplies for the hungry. After the revolution, conditions worsened. The Soviet government began bearing down on all religious expression. Joseph Isaac found himself confronted by his fellow Jews. The *Yevsektzia,* a Jewish cell of the Communist party, prided itself on being atheistic and was determined that all other Jews follow its lead. Party members tried to bully Joseph Isaac, even by threatening his life with a loaded revolver. Unimpressed, Joseph Isaac flung the financial resources of the Chabad brotherhood, and his own organizational ability and seemingly endless reserves of energy, against the political and party machinery in an effort to preserve the rights of Jews to worship God, and failing that, to encourage continued worship in defiance of the law.

Quickly he saw that the antireligious forces in the Soviet Union were overwhelming. He responded with a dual-purposed determination: The Chabad tradition was not to be stamped out by political disaster, and the Russian Jews had to be taught how to resist government interference with their religious life. To achieve the first purpose, he sent emissaries to Poland to establish a yeshivah in Warsaw, and he began syphoning off to that center the cream of religious scholars and students. He himself stayed in the Soviet Union to lead and to organize and to inspire despite increasing danger and constant harassment. Because of his courage and steadfastness, he became the foremost leader of the Jewish religion in the Soviet Union. Illegally, stealthily, but persistently, he set up religious schools for children and adults throughout the country. When the police disbanded the schools, Joseph Isaac began again.

Finally, inevitably, like his great-great-grandfather, he found himself in a Russian prison charged with treason and brought there by the accusation of another Jew. In Joseph Isaac Schneersohn's case, however, he was guilty of the charge and proud of his guilt. He was placed in solitary confinement in the Spalerno Prison in Leningrad, and sentenced to death. He would have been executed except for forceful international protest. The diplomatic clamor continued until the Soviet government permitted him to leave the country together with his family and most of the famous Lubavitcher library.

Hurrying to Riga, Latvia, Joseph Isaac Schneersohn busied himself establishing a yeshivah there. He visited the Holy Land and returned to Europe by way of the United States; while in America, he was received by Herbert Hoover in the White House. Moving his headquarters to Warsaw, he worked to increase the number of Chabad study classes and yeshivoh throughout Poland, to make the yeshivah in Warsaw a center that would attract scholars from all over the world.

Hitler had other ideas for Warsaw. Throughout the terrible blitz, Joseph Isaac Schneersohn stayed in Warsaw overseeing the evacuation of his students and demonstrating by his example that a man who has one God and "two worlds" is not afraid of death. In the midst of terror, he watched, for the second time, his hopes and dreams and years of planning being destroyed. The bombs and human screams could not kill his faith in God, however. When Succus, the springtime ceremony, arrived, Joseph Isaac built and decorated the bower and completed the rituals as though the succession of explosions were songs in praise of God. Finally, when there was nothing left for him to do, he yielded to his followers' wishes and fled smoking Poland for the United States.

When he arrived in America, he was sixty years old. He had used up his youth and his strength in Europe, but not his will. He came here intent on creating a Torah center for Chabad to replace those that had been destroyed. Choosing Brooklyn, New York, as his headquarters, he soon established a central Lubavitch yeshivah. Old, an exjailbird, a refugee, Joseph Isaac Schneersohn was hard at work making an environment. There was not much to begin with. Everywhere he looked about him in his new home he saw laxness, compromise, forgetfulness, even ignorance of the fundamentals of Judaism.

Organizing, organizing, drawing on invisible sources of energy, he made the environment begin to happen. Bible classes took shape; so did Hebrew classes; more yeshivoh; numerous welfare organizations to heal the holes in bodies so he could begin working on souls; a publishing house that is still producing masses of printed material—books, pamphlets, newspapers, magazines, fleets of rattletrap vehicles bringing Judaism to those Jews lost in the gentile wilderness—young peoples' clubs; and more schools, schools, schools—for the young, for the old, for girls, for boys, by the day, by the hour; Rabbi Joseph Isaac Schneersohn caught Americans when he could, as many as he could, and taught them as much as they would let him. A minute, an hour, a day, a year, a lifetime—it all went into the "environment."

In all, his American years, the last of his life, were only ten. But as his body gave way, his vision broadened, and his compassion stretched to encompass all the world. And he sent his emissaries following the reach of compassion, establishing yeshivoh to train rabbis to carry on the work and, where needed, to establish technical schools to develop skills.

Whenever he heard of a need for leadership, he tried to fill it. Canada, England, France, Israel, Australia, Eastern Europe—all have benefited from his schools. At the end of World War II, he established a special group to help those in displaced-person camps to find a country in which to live and to train for a profession by which to live. His efforts and financing built two villages for refugees in Israel. And finally, as the end of that last ten-year period came, he discovered a new challenge: "There is much to be done in North Africa," he told his followers. "The Jews of Morocco need teachers and guides. . . ."

Organizing, organizing until the very end.

But the organizer was also a mystic. Like the Besht, Joseph Isaac Schneersohn saw God in everything, and like the founder of Chabad, he believed that everything was part of God's planning, the unfolding of His creation. And so to him the dignity, the individuality of each thing was precious. He used in his teachings a personal torah that his father Sholom Dov Baer gave to him one sun-warmed day when they were walking together in a field of ripening grain. As they talked, Joseph Isaac, only a boy then, had absent-mindedly torn off a leaf, shredded it, and tossed it away. Seeing this, his father asked him gently if it were right to regard the work of God so lightly. "In what way," his father inquired, "is the I of the leaf less than your I." And he went on to point out that everything that exists has its own purpose and its own obligation to accomplish something.

It is easy to believe that Joseph Isaac had been born a mystic, for it is hard to see when he would have found the time to achieve mysticism. What he was he gave to the world; the purpose and the obligation he was born with had a splended fulfillment.

His successor, Menahem Mendel Schneersohn, though a direct descendant of Shneur Zalman, was not of Joseph Isaac's flesh but the husband of one of his daughters. Young Joseph Isaac, at his father's elbow, had worked among mystics and lived in a town drenched in mysticism. Young Menahem Mendel studied science and electrical engineering at the Sorbonne in France. No doubt Joseph Isaac was confirmed in his future before Bar Mitzvah, but two years were required to persuade Menahem Mendel to take up where his father-in-law had left off. But strangely, the torah of the two is much alike. Like his predecessor, Menahem Mendel believes in orthodoxy first, then mysticism.

Before trying to interest students in Chabad, he urges them to obey the six hundred thirteen ancient obligations of their religion—to keep the Sabbath and holy days, to observe family purity, to eat only ritually clean food, to put on *tefillin* (of this more in a bit), even to practice such seeming minutia as to wash hands before meals.

One of his disciples puts it this way: You must observe the commandments in order to understand Hasidism. The body effects the mind. If the body does not perform its "lessons," how can the mind learn?

So the circle has become complete. The Besht founded a sect of form-disregarding radicals who scandalized the orthodox by teaching the relationship to God was all-important. Prayer, devotion, devekut—clinging to God—superseded the prescriptions of ritual, and rules could safely be ignored by those who concentrated their thoughts on God. And here in the United States more than two hundred years later, one of his spiritual descendants calls for ritual and rule as prerequisites of mysticism.

If this seems more a betrayal than an irony, we should examine the environments in which the two lived and worked. The Besht was teaching in a land that had become crazed by form. Ritual and religious sophistry were consuming the energy of the elite and acting as a barrier between the peasants and spiritual progress. But the contemporary American scene is a miasma of formlessness, and this situation is especially true in the area of religion where many temples as well as Christian churches have become so "liberal" that leaders and congregations alike have largely ceased to deal with God, in favor of social issues.

It is said that on the day the Besht had captured, with his tales, the congregation of Jacob Joseph, he told his prospective disciple, who had been afflicted of late with painful bouts of depression, the story of a peasant and his team of horses. The peasant thought it would be a grand-sounding thing if his horses whinnied as they ran. He pulled at the reins to force his horses to whinny. Their ears pulled back, but they made no sound. He pulled harder, again and again. Still no sound. Finally, he gave up and slackened the reins. Then the horses neighed. Jacob Joseph had been pulling the reins too hard, too hard on himself and too hard on his congregation.

In America, however, the horses were not even harnessed and moving. The Lubavitcher rabbis feel that to protect religious belief before the onslaught of contemporary materialism, discipline is needed as is strict observation of Jewish law—first form, then formlessness, first the mitzvoh, then the more heady mysticism.

The Lubavitcher leadership is consistent in taking its cue from the environment as to what aspects of Hasidism to stress or withhold. Shneur Zalman, living in an age when Hasidic miracles were common, had discouraged the practice of the occult. But here in rationalistic America in the last half of the twentieth century, few people believe a miracle is possible unless it comes out of a test tube. Here children are taught to believe only what they can see with their eyes and feel with their hands. And so, to sweeten their discipline, to demonstrate that there are other worlds and other spheres, to make an environment, the Schneersohn rebbes do a little wonder-working.

But like his predecessor, Menahem Mendel is his greatest wonder. He confers with those who wish to see him from the evening hours sometimes until the break of day. Those are long hours, but all the Chabad Hasidim are welcomed when they come to him with their problems. During the day, he continues Joseph Isaac Schneersohn's work of organizing. He has time for everyone and everything. He never seems rushed or hurried. And he never seems to sleep.

The work progresses.

One would think that the uncompromising attitude of the Schneersohn rebbes regarding orthodox discipline would alienate from them the impatient young, but the reverse is true. Menahem Mendel has an army of young men and women working for him, hundreds of young emissaries throughout America. They are his hands and feet. They repeat his torah. They go out in pairs across the nation's highways to urge Jews to observe the high holy days and to follow at least some of the mitzvoh. They man his bookstores, selling the Lubavitcher texts and pamphlets. They are the enterprising sales force of the famous Lubavitcher tefillin campaign. When a political issue comes up that draws Lubavitcher attention, his young people do the footwork, the dull scrub work that show up in votes and are making New York's professional politicians look at the Lubavitcher Hasidim with respectful eyes. And they are the crucial, living communication link with the bored young intellectuals who are into dope or communal marriages or Krishna consciousness or the Jesus-freak movement or one form or another of revolutionary activism.

Some of Menahem Mendel's young army wear the long earlocks and round brimmed hats that have become the insignia of Hasidim, but others look much like the newcomers they bring to their rabbis, occasionally even to the red-rimmed eyes—the newcomers from pot and heavy drinking, the young Chabad Hasidim from a bout of lengthy praying. But the emotional differences between the two are great enough to be perceived. For this reason, many who came to one of the services for a trip or a kick have become regulars.

In a sense Chabad Hasidism is a trip. One of the regulars said of a class in mysticism, "You don't walk home, you fly." A real relationship with God has been a missing ingredient in American life. Those who go to the services, who attend the classes, find something they have never had before.

Praying is hard, serious work, but it is heady work, too. In trying to communicate what they feel, mystics have often resorted to the language of chemical inebriation, just as they have often used sexual imagery: drunk, ecstatic, intoxicated, high, trembling, on fire, dizzy, piercing love, swooning. Mystics have "bad trips," too, moments of the deepest despair, hopelessness, and worthlessness, so that the young people who are leaving the drug culture behind do not find they are giving up excitement for a sterile existence. The opposite is true. Quickly their old life seems boring to them compared to the increased excitement of their life in the Chabad movement.

What is new to them is the purpose and responsibility of their new role. Rebbe Mcnahem Mendel uses his young followers. He thinks of them as men and women and he trusts them to work like men and women. The trust brings with it a sense of personal dignity and a sense of adventure. They begin to feel that their lives have meaning, that they are capable of changing society.

The purpose and sense of dignity alone have kept scores of young people persevering in the disciplines of Chabad when they have never stuck to anything before in their lives. Often the commitment is to a specific rabbi rather than to the movement—"I wouldn't want to let Rabbi —— down." This commitment after all is one of the advantages of the masterdisciple relationship: the novice will do for his teacher what he could not do for himself.

Chabad Houses have been springing up like mushrooms across the nation, usually close to a university or college. Blending into the neighborhood scene, they are a contemporary version of the eastern European Hasidic stibble, providing a place to worship, a homey atmosphere in which to visit with friends, a study, a dining hall for communal eating, and even a place for sleeping. The proliferation of Chabad Houses is so rapid that when asked for a national count, a young Lubavitcher rolls his eyes at the effort to give an up-to-date number for the state.

Open to everyone, the front doors at the Chabad Houses are never locked. Young and old, Gentile and Jew, orthodox and atheist, make their way through the door. Some come to learn, and occasionally some come to scoff, for such is the way of our times; some come to break windows or even steal. The rabbis in charge of the Chabad Houses seem to have much the same ability to read character and intent in the face as did the Hasidim of old. They neither denounce nor turn away those who come for a lark or to scoff, but somehow such purposes change or the alien leaves. Only those bent on destruction are actively made unwelcome.

In the Chabad House, welcoming in the Sabbath—which according to Jewish reckoning is not Sunday but Saturday— begins Friday evening shortly before sundown, when the young college women, dressed in short wool skirts and shapely tops, perform the ritual of lighting the Sabbath candles. When the candles have been lit, the man who will lead the service comes into the main hall. There Hasidim and novices, young and old, are seated, waiting, chatting.

"Come on," the leader says. "The women have finished with the candles, but there's time before the week ends to get in a few more mitzvoh. Is there anyone here who has not put on tefillin?" A few may indicate that they are candidates, and the leader helps them with the ritual. The leader looks to be no more than eighteen despite his full beard and long black coat. For the Sabbath he is wearing a "second covering," a black snap brim hat over his yarmulke.

As soon as the two men have finished observing tefillin, the leader begins the services. Despite the emphasis on orthodox procedure, there is much Hasidic spontaneity in the praying. The leader begins loudly, but quickly reverts to a volume intended for himself and God, from time to time speaking up again to let the others know where he is in the service. Not that they seem to care. Each person proceeds at his own rate and in his own praying voice that is natural for him. Some look out of the window as they pray. Some thump the furniture; others clap their hands. Most of them move heads or torsos in a rhythmic swaying to the beat of their chanting.

The women are upstairs in the balcony, separated from the men by distance, an ancient tradition. Even these women of the liberation generation who speak determinedly of their future plans have no objection to this segregation. "I prefer to *daaven* (pray) with the women. I find I can concentrate better if I am not physically close to my boyfriend."

Then after, the first portion of the service, couches are dragged around the main room to form two lines facing each other, men on one side, women on the other. At the head of the row, with his back to the fireplace, the rabbi begins his interpretation of the week's portion of the Torah. First he translates a passage from the Hebrew; then he gives his own interpretation in English.

The rabbis speak Yiddish among themselves; Yiddish has remained the home language of the Schneersohn family and of the most intimate circle of disciples. It would be lovely to believe that among the contributions of Chabad Hasidism will be the preservation of Yiddish as a spoken language, but probably that is too large a miracle for even them to accomplish. Our multitudinous language system is as endangered as the earth's wildlife; we seem to be rushing headlong to a drab few species, a one-tongued world. It will be a sorry event when the libraries of spiritual writing, the literature, and the humor of Yiddish is lost to all but a few scholars.

The Torah—the first five books of the Bible: Genesis, Exodus, Leviticus, Numbers, and Deuteronomy—is broken into portions and read in Hebrew in solemn ceremony, one portion per week during the year. On the holiday that commemorates God's giving His Torah to the Jewish people, the scroll on which the Torah is written is rewound back to the first line: "In the beginning. . . ." The ceremonial reading has taken place earlier in the week. The informal study class devotes most of the time to English commentaries of the Talmud and the Mishnah and other texts, and the rabbi explains their interpretations, especially those that seem to be conflicting, and develops his application of the Torah to the world today and the lives of his listeners.

When this part of the period is finished, the rabbi asks the group for questions and discussion. It is lively, challenging, and informal. Stories are told. Jokes are made. Social and political lessons are drawn.

During one such service, the Torah portion dealt with Exodus, and the rabbi told how the frightened Jews fleeing from the Pharaoh of Egypt had been trapped between the Egyptian army and the Red Sea and were arguing about what to do. Some wanted to surrender to the Egyptians. Some preferred death to more life as a slave. Then one man, a common man, not a judge or a rabbi, did just what God had commanded. He went into the sea. He walked up to his waist in the waters. Then up to his neck. He continued walking steadily until the water was just below his nose and if he went any farther, he would not be able to breathe. But he took that next step. And as he did, the waters parted. God had worked the miracle he promised. The rest of the Jews were able to cross the sea without even getting wet.

Commenting, the rabbi said, "A Jew must trust his God. If God says: 'Go into the sea,' you go into the sea. No questions. No fooling around. You go."

Then the rabbi went on to the section in which the Egyptian army tried to follow after the Jews, using the passage God had created, but God caused the waters to close down on them, drowning the Egyptians. Seeing this closing from the far shore, the Jews were hurrahing the deaths of their former slavemasters. And God asked them: Why are you cheering the destruction of my creations? And the Jews were rebuked.

Perhaps few sections of the Bible hold a more pertinent message for our own times than does this one. And this point of view is one that the Besht stressed. In one of the tales about him, he says, "Let no man think himself better than his neighbor, for all serve God, each according to the measure of understanding which God has given him."

Throughout the first part of the service and the Torah study class late arrivals had been straggling in. No one seemed to object to the distractions. No one, including the rabbi, seemed to feel they were "late." They were welcomed with warm smiles, and people moved over on the sofas or drew up a chair to make room for them. When the discussion period had ended, the benches and seats were rearranged, the men and women moving quickly but casually, as though they were accustomed to converting this hall to accommodate many uses. This time solid screens were placed down the center of the room, once again separating the men and women, and the service was resumed with more daavening and singing.

At the end of the Sabbath service, the screens were removed and the furniture was pushed back to make room for dancing. The men and women formed separate circles and the dancing began. Round and round the circles went, the dancers moving vigorously, singing loudly, shouting and laughing. In the center of the men's circle, two men linked arms, dancing expertly; the pace quickened and their agility increased. The rhythm and melody of the song and dance were traditionally Hasidic. When the steps permitted, there was much clapping. Several young men somersaulted on the floor from one side of the circle to the other. The tone and temper of the music, the singing and dancing, and the somersaults were exciting and joyous, but a bit disconcerting for those who associate religion with solemn faces.

When the dancing was over—the youngest and strongest panting and wiping their foreheads—the singing didn't stop. While the room was once again put back into shape, everyone shook hands and wished each other, "Good Sabbath! Good Sabbath!" Still singing traditional songs, the group moved on to the dining hall upstairs.

The same coeds who had participated in the candle-lighting ceremony had cooked the meal and were bringing it in courses to the table. The dancing made for good appetite; everyone sat down and began to eat heartily. The meal was traditional: bread and wine, a serving of gefilte fish, the salad with lots of greens and a delicious dressing, and the last course, a handsome serving of juicy chicken.

There was more conversation and laughter while the dishes were being washed and the dining hall straightened up. But even then the evening was not finished for those living beyond walking distance to Chabad House. In the orthodox tradition, it is forbidden to ride on the Sabbath. Sleeping bags were brought out and Chabad House became, in addition to all of its other functions, a hostel.

The young Chabad Hasidim carry out their rebbe's tefillin campaign with the same zest that goes into their dancing. Shortly before the Six Day War, Jews and their friends around the world were holding their breath, wondering if Israel could survive the massive attack of the Arab nations. Some sent munitions. Some sent money to help Israel. Some sent volunteers. The Lubavitchers sent mitzvoh—the tefillin campaign: "A Jew must trust his God. If God says, 'Go into the sea,' you go into the sea. No questions. No fooling around. You go." It was a mystic's response, but a mystic who is also a warrior. Of the six hundred thirteen possible mitzvoh, observation of tefillin was chosen because it was the one that carried the promise of striking terror into the hearts of Israel's enemies.

Tefillin is the name for two leather boxes that hold pieces of parchment on which a person who has qualified for this privilege has inscribed four sections of the Torah: Deuteronomy 6:4-9 and 11:13-21, and Exodus 13:1-10 and 13:11-16. The contents of these passages express the monotheism of Judaism—"Hear O Israel, God our Lord, God is One!"—His promise to reward those who obey His precepts and His promise to punish those who do not; Israel's duty to remember the redemption from Egyptian bondage; and the obligation upon the parents to pass on this information to their children.

One of the boxes is bound to the left arm by leather straps in such a manner that the box will rest against the heart and the other is bound so that it rests against the head. In this way the head, the heart, and the hand are incorporated in prayer, bringing into focus the dedication to God of all one thinks, and feels, and does. Basic to Chabad Hasidism is the necessity of the intellect to control the emotions. The gulf between the two is lamented, but by observing the commandment to put on tefillin, the convergence of mind and heart can be assisted. Ritual rigidly governs the entire ceremony of observing tefillin. For this reason many American Jews have rebelled against this ancient tradition. Liberal Jews are more likely to speak of tefillin with embarrassment or irritation than with neutrality.

Nevertheless, when Rebbe Menahem Mendel sent out the call to Jews over the world to observe the mitzvah of tefillin, tefillin booths sprang up in cities where there were Chabad Hasidim: New York, London, Tel Aviv, Los Angeles, Melbourne, and dozens of smaller ones. From the cities tefillin vans and buses rolled the highways to small towns and farmlands. No one knows how many Jews observed the tefillin before the first gunshot of the Six Day War.

Was the tefillin campaign in any way related to the Israeli victory? That question has been asked more than once. And more than once the answer is a smile and another question: Did you expect the war to end in six days?

Although victory was achieved, the campaign goes on. As soon as the sacred Wailing Wall was liberated from Arab territory, Chabad Hasidim set up a permanent tefillin post so that Jews visiting the holy place would be able to observe the mitzvah. More than one-half million Jews in half a year have wrapped the leather straps according to the ancient tradition—many for the first time in their lives.

In Los Angeles on the sidewalk outside the Chabad's Midcity Center storefront, a young Hasid inquires of a passing male pedestrian, "Are you Jewish?" If the answer is yes, the smiling Hasid gently steers his charge inside, asking, "Would you like to put on the tefillin?"

The Rebbe has discovered the campaign is winning another war: that of indifference. Once a person has observed one mitzvah, the second one comes more easily. And the Rebbe makes the point, "We will have no future unless our past is vitally present." And so the Los Angeles scene is repeated across the nation, around the world.

When the Hasidim find their prospect is hesitant to take that first step, they are apt to remind him of the torah of the mystic, Moses Maimonides: Every man should look upon himself as if he had completed half good deeds and half evil ones, so that the sums exactly balance. And he should look at the world the same way, as though it balanced half evil, half good. So one single mitzvah can tip the balance to the favorable side for the man who observed the mitzvah and through him for the entire world.

One act. Ten minutes of your life given against the chance of saving yourself and the world in the bargain. It is an equation that even agnostics find irresistible. The appeal is strong to our sense of the heroic, to our spirit of adventure and daring, and, on a lower level, to the gambler in us. A simple act, a moment's gamble, easily accomplished, quickly completed, but perhaps it is only the beginning.

And so there you have the Hasidim: more than two hundred years of mystics captured in print, their knowledge and being available to us, as is the promise that the process of this approach to mysticism is going on, not barely surviving, but bursting in mystical vitality so that we may observe or become a part of it. We are watching, some of us already a part, some of us yet to become part of a new era of spiritual excitement and achievement.

Much of the living reality of even the contemporary Hasidim has been lost and distorted in the telling. That is a sorry fact. And the fact handicaps those who need histories as patterns for their own efforts, but what is done cannot be undone. We can be glad for what we have, and use what we have, do what we can, and ready ourselves for more guidance and better patterns when the time is right. But can the Hasidic patterns be effective when they seem to be so conflicting? Their usefulness and their credibility as effective patterns come from this variability. People come in diverse types; one size does not fit all. Historical periods are almost as diverse as people. One pattern would not be useful to the needs of each age. Only a dead language has unchanging rules of grammar and a set vocabulary. Only a dead discipline never varies in its approach.

Hasidism is still growing, still changing to meet the needs of a new generation. And in this present generation, which has so many differing types, differing starting points in their religious search, the variety of methods, which the lives of the Hasidim illustrate, suggest that there may be a pattern for each of us.

Not everyone is ready for the discipline of conforming to the orthodox tradition required to take advantage of Chabad Hasidism's invitation to all Jews. Hopefully, not everyone who reads this book is a Jew or feels the need to become a Jew.

Liberal, conservative, orthodox, Jew, Christian, Hindu, Mohammedan—the lives and torah of mystics speak to us all.

The responsibility to listen and to choose what we need from the patterns they offer is ours. Suppose we choose wrongly?

Perhaps, especially today, the choosing is more important than the choice. Making a commitment, a beginning, is wiser than scrupulosity. One common theme throughout the lives of the Hasidic mystics is the time and the effort they put into their search and the frequent uncertainty as to proper direction.

The search for God is full of dangers and wrong turns, but at least it is never dull. And if the searcher presses on, the wrong turn eventually becomes the right turn. One torah of the Hasidic mystics which we can all accept is that the place to start is where you are at. Don't look backward with regret, but forward with joy and resolution.

Glossary

Aaron ben Jacob of Karlin: Disciple of Dov Baer; a zaddik who emphasized asceticism, sin, and scholarship; the first to establish Hasidism in Lithuania.

Aryeh Leib Sarahs: One of Dov Baer's disciples who maintained the life-style of an ancient Jewish mystic.

Baal Shem Tov: (literally, Master of the Good Name) A title given to Israel ben Eliezer, the founder of Hasidism. Also spelled Ball Shem Tob, Ba'al Shem Tov, Baalshem, and abbreviated to the Besht, a nickname by which Israel ben Eliezer was often called.

baal shem: (literally, master of the name) A title given to a host of healers who used the magical power of the names of God and power derived from manipulation of numeric values of the letters in the names of God to achieve cures. *See Tetragrammaton.*

Bar Mitzvah: (literally, son of commandment) A Jewish male who, having reached the age of thirteen years, is considered an adult obligated to observe God's commandments and to take his place in the religious activity of the community; a ceremony celebrating a boy's thirteenth birthday.

Beinoni: (literally, the average man) Used by Shneur Zalman in contradistinction to a man with inborn spiritual greatness. Shneur Zalman designed the rules and methodology of Chabad Hasidism for the beinoni rather than for the saint.

Besht: Abbreviation of Baal Shem Tov, which see.

Chabad: (literally, an acrostic for Chochma [concept] *, Binah* [understanding] *, Daat [concentration] + carrying the idea or chochma to its conclusion)* The brotherhood or methodology founded by Shneur Zalman of the Hasidic movement. Also spelled Habad.

Chasid (pl. Chasidim): See Hasid.

Chasidism: See Hasidism.

Cheder: See Heder.

Daaven: To pray.

Devekut: (literally, clinging) A spiritual state in which the thoughts and emotions of the worshiper are unwaveringly "attached" to God.

Dov Baer: Disciple of the Besht who eventually assumed the leadership of the Hasidic movement following the Besht's death.

Ein Soph: God in Himself; the unknowable totality of God's being.

Elimelech of Lyzhansk: A disciple of Dov Baer; noted for his occult powers and mystical devotion.

Jacob Frank: Founder of Jewish sect in the eighteenth century which openly opposed the Talmud, joining forces with the Christian clergy in their fight against Jewish orthodoxy. Eventually most of his followers converted to Catholicism and the movement died out.

Frankist: See above.

Galuth: (literally, exile) A word of great emotional significance within Judaism, carrying several layers of meaning. Originally it referred to the (pre-1948) fact that the Jewish people had lost their homeland and as a people without a nation of their own were forced to dwell in the territories of strangers and their enemies. The word came to have meaning within mystical thought of this period in which the individual souls appear to be caught on the materialistic plane and

have lost their sense of identity with God, a period
which will end with the coming of the Messiah. The
Lubavitcher leader, Rabbi Menahem Mendel, has used
the word in the interesting and beautiful way of being
in exile from one's essential self, referring specifically
to the Jewish person who turns religious beliefs and
customs of his people (which are a part of him on
deep emotional levels) in order to conform to the
values of materialism or the world of the Gentiles.

Gentile: A non-Jew; non-Jewish.

Gaon or Great Gaon: See Elijah the Gaon of Wilna.

Heder: Religious school for young children in east European
Jewish communities. Often the school was held in a
room of the teacher's house.

Phenehas Horowitz: In his youth influenced by Dov Baer and
other Hasidic teachers; as a prosperous rabbi in
Germany he became estranged from and antagonistic
to Hasidism; brother of Samuel Horowitz.

Samuel Shnelke Horowitz: In his youth a student of Dov
Baer and other Hasidic teachers; a Hasidic sympa-
thizer and recruiter, but never really a member of the
brotherhood.

Iluy: (literally, exalted) An affectionate title given to a brilliant young scholar of the Talmud; a prodigy; a boy
genius.

Infidel: A Gentile; a non-Jew.

Jacob Isaac ben Asher: A disciple of Jacob Isaac the Seer; the
founder of Przysucha Hasidim, a brotherhood and
methodology which emphasized scholarship and discipline and renounced the use of occult powers.

Jacob Isaac the Seer of Lublin: A disciple of Dov Baer and of
Elimelech of Lyzhansk; a zaddik who rejected talmudic scholarship in favor of devotion; famous for the
use of his occult powers to help the material condition of his followers.

Israel: The name given to Jacob as the ancestor of the Hebrews and hence the spirit of the Jewish people or the totality of Jewish people (wherever they might be living) at a given time; the territory of their historic homeland—this land is sacred to the Jewish people and possesses in itself mystical powers because it was there that God revealed their special relationship to Him as a chosen people and their obligations (mitzvoh) to Him due to this relationship, hence the Holy Land; the Republic of Israel with politically agreed upon national territorial borders.

Israel ben Eliezer: See Baal Shem Tov.

Israel ben Shabbetai: A disciple of Dov Baer; a zaddik and an exponent of practical zaddikism. *See Practical Zaddikism.*

Kabbalah: (literally, received tradition) The accumulated mystical doctrines and their systems handed down through generations of Jewish mystics, some going back beyond historical time and hence including parts of the Torah, and others referring only to the doctrines and systems originating from the twelfth century on; the prime source of Jewish mysticism. Also spelled Kabalah, Kabbala, Chabbalah, cabala, etc.

Kaddish: A type of prayer; best known for its use as a prayer for the souls of the dead.

Kavanah: A spiritual state sometimes achieved only briefly during meditation and prayer in which one's thoughts and emotions are focused or concentrated upon God. Also spelled kavvanah.

Kugel: Noodle pudding.

Lubavitcher: (literally, referring to the town of Lubavitch in White Russia) A member of the Chabad Hasidim established by Shneur Zalman which first became famous when the brotherhood was located in the town of Lubavitch. Today the headquarters of the Chabad Hasidim is in the Crown Heights section of Brooklyn, N.Y.

Luria, Isaac: A greatly influential sixteenth-century Kabbalistic scholar. Also known as Ari (lion) or the Great Ari.

Maggid or the Maggid of Meseritz: (literally, preacher) A title given to Dov Baer by which he was commonly called. *See Dov Baer.*

maggid (pl. maggidim): A popular preacher prevalent in eastern Europe in the seventeenth and eighteenth centuries famous for the length of their exhortations.

Medziboz: Town in which the Besht had his headquarters during the height of his fame.

Rebbe Menahem Mendel of Brooklyn: The current leader of the Chabad Hasidim. *See Chabad and Lubavitcher.*

Rabbi Menahem Mendel of Permyshlany: Disciple of Dov Baer; for a time assumed leadership of the Hasidic brotherhood, later established a Hasidic conventicle in the Holy Land.

Meseritz: Town in which Dov Baer (the Maggid) had his headquarters during the height of his fame.

Messiah: The One Who will be the Redeemer and the Ruler of Israel at the climax of human history and Who is the Instrument by which the Kingdom of God will be established.

Mikvah: Pool or tub for immersion in water in a ritual of purification. Also spelled mikveh.

Minyan: (literally, quorum) A group of at least ten adult (aged 13 or over) Jewish males that is necessary to begin a liturgical service. Hence, colloquially, a synagogue or place of worship, especially if the place is makeshift.

Mishnah: The core of oral law compiled on the basis of previous collections and codified around 200 A.D.

Mitzvah (pl. mitzvoh): (literally, commandment) Religious obligations as set forth in the Torah. There are 613 mitzvoh in the Torah. In U.S.A., colloquially has come to mean a blessing because observing a mitzvah brings about a blessing. *See Bar Mitzvah.*

Nachman ben Ssimha: Great-grandchild of the Baal Shem
Tov; a zaddik; famous as a storyteller.

Natham of Nemerov: Disciple of Nachman ben Ssimha;
responsible for writing down and publishing Rabbi
Nachman's tales.

Orthodox: The branch of Judaism that adheres to the Mosaic
law as interpreted in the Talmud; adhering to Orthodox Judaism.

Phylacteries: See Tefillin.

Pidyonat: (literally, ransom) Money given, according to
Hasidic custom, to the zaddik by one of his followers
together with a request for material or spiritual assist-
ance that has been written on a slip of paper. The gift
ransoms the request.

Practical Kabbalah: The parts of the Kabbalah dealing with
occultism; the systems of occultism based on Kabbalistic knowledge. *See Kabbalah.*

Practical Zaddikism: The theory which states it is part of a
zaddik's responsibility to his followers to use his
occult powers to help their material welfare (in the
belief that spiritual development cannot occur on a
foundation of misery); practical zaddikism is also
noted for the emphasis on the exalted spiritual state
of the zaddik and the extreme devotion almost to the
point of idolatry his followers feel for their zaddik.

Rabbi: A title given to an ordained teacher of Jewish law
authorized to issue decisions in religious and ritualistic matters and to perform marriages and other
liturgical services. Unfortunately in the seventeenth
and eighteenth centuries in Europe it was used
loosely as a title of respect for any religious scholar or
holy person.

Rav: (literally, teacher) The Rav is one of the titles by which
Shneur Zalman was called by his followers.

Rebbe: Title for a Hasidic zaddik; the spiritual leader of a
Hasidic dynasty or brotherhood.

Rosh Hashanah: The first day of the New Year according to the Jewish calendar; a two-day festival at the beginning of the month of Tishri celebrating the New Year, which falls between September and October of the Gregorian calendar.

Sefirah (pl. Sefirot): A fundamental concept of the Kabbalists originating in the ten primordial or ideal numbers; hence the ten stages of emanation that emerged from the Ein Soph and form the realm of God's manifestation. Each Sefirah is related to an aspect of God. The totality of ten Sefirot form the Tree of Life, a dynamic unity in which the activity of God reveals itself; the rhythms of its unfolding are the rhythms of creation. The mystical archtypes for the existence of the world.

Shalom Aleichem: Hebrew greeting meaning "Peace be unto You."

Shamus: Beadle; an assistant to the rabbi; guardian of the Torah. Also spelled shamash, shammash.

Shekhinah: Numinous emanation of God in the world; the presence of God in the life of man and the community—it was largely in this sense that the Besht and many of the other Hasidic teachers emphasizing devotion rather than talmudic scholarship used the term; in the Kabbalah the Shekhinah is the tenth Sefirah and represents the feminine principle, the feminine aspect of divinity. Also spelled Shekinah, Shekina, Sechinnah, etc.

Shirayim: (literally, remains) Food a zaddik has tasted and by virtue of this contact confers a blessing or spiritual uplifting upon the consumer.

Stibble: A place of worship that was also used as a community center and hostel by the early Hasidim.

Succus: Feast of Tabernacles. A seven-day holiday starting on the fifteenth day of Tishri of the Jewish calendar, falling between September and October of the

Gregorian calendar which commemorates the temporary shelter the Jews had during their wandering in the desert and celebrates the gathering of the harvest. It is customary to build a temporary shelter for the Succus. Also spelled Sukkoth.

Synagogue: A building for worship and religious instruction for a congregation of Jews and presided over by a rabbi. However, the synagogue belongs to the congregation who hire the rabbi and can dismiss him if they wish.

Talmud: Postbiblical rabbinical law consisting of the Mishnah and the Gemorro. The Palestinian and Babylonian Talmuds are the two famous compilations of the discussions and interpretations of oral law.

Talmudic scholar: A man well versed in the Talmuds and their many subsequent interpretations. A brilliant mind, a retentive mind, and years of intensive study are required to achieve the necessary proficiency.

Tanya: A famous book by Shneur Zalman in which he expounds the principles of Chabad. This is a nickname taken from the book's first word; its official title is *Likute Amorim.*

Tefillin: Two black leather cubes fastened to leather straps and containing four passages from the Pentateuch written on parchment (Exodus 13:1-10; 13:11-16; Deuteronomy 6:4-9; 11:13-21). An error in the written text or transcription by an unauthorized person nullifies the blessing of the tefillin. The tefillin are placed on the left arm and the forehead during the weekday morning service, and at any time during the weekday by those participating in the Lubavitcher tefillin campaign but never on Sabbath and holy days.

Temple: Synagogue, which see.

Tetragrammaton: An ancient Israelite name for God. The quadriliteral name of God referred to in Josephus, in the magic papyri, and in the Palestinian Talmud. God in his essence, the absolute, nonderivative, non-compositive state which transcends revelation and is the source of manifestation; the infinite God who transcends space and time and is beyond creation and Nature. God the Unknowable. Hence Tetragrammaton is a particularly holy and powerful name. In mystical and occult systems knowledge of how to pronounce this name properly was the source of great power.

Tikun: Money for support of young men living in the zaddik's court to serve him and study under him.

Torah: The first five books of the Bible, which Moses received from God; often refers to the entire Jewish law including the Talmud and other sacred literature.

torah: Teaching; to give torah; to teach.

Yarmulke: A skullcap worn by orthodox Jews in observance of the obligation to keep the head covered before the Lord. Also spelled yamulke.

Yeshivah: A center of Jewish higher education in which young men study the Torah, the Talmud, and other religious literature.

Yiddish: A hybrid language of Hebrew and German with additions from a variety of eastern European languages using the Hebrew alphabet. Recently Yiddish writing has used the Roman alphabet.

Yihud (pl. yihudim): Mystical incantations utilizing the Names of God in special combination used along with meditational exercises designed to bring about the union of God and his Shekhinah.

Levi Yitzhok: A disciple of Dov Baer; a Hasidic teacher famous for his love of the poor, his innocence, and his devotion to God.

Yom Kippur: The Day of Atonement; a day set aside in the Jewish calendar for fasting, repentance of sins, and prayer.

Yoshbi: A disciple of a zaddik who lives in the zaddik's court and devotes his time to serving the zaddik and studying under his direction; usually a young man.

Zaddik (pl. zaddikim): (literally, righteous) The leader of a Hasidic brotherhood or dynasty. Also spelled tsaddik, tzaddik, zadik, etc.

Shneur Zalman: A famous disciple of Dov Baer; founder of Chabad Hasidism. Also spelled Shenier Zalman.

Sabbatai Zevi: A seventeenth-century Jewish adventurer who fraudulently proclaimed himself to be the Messiah and thereby attained for a while a large and excited following.

Zeddakah: (literally, benevolence) Systematic activity in community welfare; a discipline proposed by Shneur Zalman as being as useful as prayer in achieving devotion to God.

Zimzum: A doctrine originated by Isaac Luria to explain and to synthesize the concept of the creation and existence of this material world and the concept of an infinite God, Who is in himself all being, precluding any existence outside himself as an infringement on his infinity. In order to allow creation of the universe to take place God contracted or condensed or concentrated himself in a planned progression. The ultimate goal is the spiritual uplifting of creation to the point that it can be united with and conscious of the Infinite without losing its identity. Shneur Zalman took this doctrine, modifying it somewhat in terms of philosophic content, but most important, applied it to his teaching so that Chabad education attempts to bring the student through an orderly series of progressions in an opposite or upward direction from the initial condensation toward the ultimate goal.

Zohar: (literally, brightness) A principal work of the Kabbalah by Simeon ben Yohai, often called in English the Book of Splendor. It contains commentaries and interpretations of the Torah, prayers, doctrines of spiritual life, teachings about creation, the human soul, and the search for God.

Meshulam Zusya of Hanipoli: Disciple of Dov Baer, brother of Elimelech of Lyzhansk; one of the great heroes of Hasidic folk tales.

Reading List

Ben-Amos, Dan, and Mintz, Jerome R., eds. and transls. *In Praise of the Baal Shem Tov:* The Earliest Collection of Legends about the Founder of Hasidism. Bloomington, Ind.: Indiana University Press, 1972.

A delightful way to become acquainted with the genre of the Hasidic folk tale and to catch a glimpse of the Besht through the eyes of those who knew him. Also contains a magnificent bibliography for those who have become interested in the history and environment related to the Besht.

Buber, Martin. *The Tales of Rabbi Nachman.* Translated by Maurice Friedman. Paperback. Bloomington, Ind.: Indiana University Press, 1962, and New York: Discus Books, 1970.

Buber's short essay on Jewish mysticism is valuable in itself and his handling of the Nachman tales is the work of a master craftsman.

Buber, Martin. *The Way of Man According to the Teaching of Hasidism.* London: Vincent Stuart, 1963.

This book more than any other is responsible for the association of Buber and Hasidism. I was tempted to include a discussion of Buber in the text because he represents a well known, contemporary example of the synthesis of Hasidic thought and fervor with an urban life-style. Ultimately, I refrained because, as an interpreter and admirer of Hasidism, not a practicing Hasid, he is aside from the central theme of this book.

Buber, Martin. *I and Thou.* Translated by Walter Kaufman. New York: Charles Scribner's Sons, 1970.

Not a book devoted to Hasidism, but one representing the Buber synthesis of Jewish traditions and written in the marvelous Buber manner.

Chagall, Marc. *The Hasidim.* New York: Crown Publishers, 1970.

The European Hasidim as seen by a great artist; I wish some museum or art society would sponsor a tour of the originals, but in the meantime Crown Publishers has done us all a service.

Cohen, Arthur. *A People Apart: Hasidism in America.* Photography by Philip Garvin. New York: E. P. Dutton & Co., 1970.

Don't miss this one; nothing can replace the visual and Mr. Garvin has a sensitive eye.

Newman, L. I., ed. *The Hasidic Anthology.* New York: Schocken Books, 1963.

A sampler and like any appetizer a bit of a tease.

Weiner, Hebert. *9½ Mystics: The Kabbala Today.* Paperback. New York: Collier Books, 1971.

I really shouldn't put you on to this one. I've read it beyond counting and each time I grow sick with jealousy. Weiner is such a delight that the information is part of you before you realize you're being educated.

The Chabad—Lubavitcher—bookstores have a wealth of inexpensive pamphlets and books, magazines and newspapers (from ten cents to a few dollars). There you can obtain an English translation of *Tanya*, a study of the pre-Hasidic Lubavitcher mystics, works by the Schneersohn rebbes, short accounts of the importance of tefillin, the significance of the skull-cap, explanations of the Jewish holy days, and stories for children (which I enjoyed hugely). It's marvelous browsing and even if you go home with your arms full, you won't be broke. If the Lubavitchers haven't discovered your neighborhood yet, you can send away for a free catalogue by writing to:

Kehot Publication Society
770 Eastern Parkway
Brooklyn, N.Y. 11213

The "For the Millions" Series